FRESH
EXPRESSIONS

FRESH
EXPRESSIONS

A New Kind of Methodist Church for People Not in Church

Kenneth H. Carter Jr. and Audrey Warren

Abingdon Press™
Nashville

FRESH EXPRESSIONS:
A NEW KIND OF METHODIST CHURCH FOR PEOPLE NOT IN CHURCH

Copyright © 2017 by Abingdon Press

Library of Congress Cataloging-in-Publication Data has been requested.

ISBN 978-1-5018-4920-6

For further information from the authors about Fresh Expressions in the USA, visit http://www.flumc.org/freshexpressions and http://freshexpressionsus.org/.

17 18 19 20 21 22 23 24 25 26—10 9 8 7 6 5 4 3 2 1
MANUFACTURED IN THE UNITED STATES OF AMERICA

CONTENTS

PREFACE

We write as pastors who love the church, and yet we know from personal experience, observation, and the data that the fastest growing religious sector in the United States is the formerly churched and indeed those who have never entered a church building. Call them by whatever name you wish, but these are our friends, family members, children, grandchildren, neighbors, and co-workers.

Because we are *Wesleyan,* we believe that God is present in their lives. Because we are *evangelical,* we sense a calling to share the gospel with them. Because we are *United Methodist,* we are committed to the purpose of making disciples for the transformation of the world. And because we are *apostolic,* we believe that we cannot passively wait for these persons to flow into our church buildings on Sunday mornings at eleven o' clock.

Instead, we are called to go to the places—the networks, the neighborhoods, the third places—where the nones and the dones, the unchurched and the dechurched increasingly gather. We hope you will join us.

We do not want to contribute to the rhetoric of blaming and judging. There is already sufficient cynicism and criticism in the literature about the church. We want to generate a constructive conversation. We want to support the building or rebuilding of vital congregations that gather inside our buildings but also increasingly outside of them.

This has been our life's work. One of us (Audrey) has served as a leader of youth and young adults, as a transformational pastor of a profoundly multicultural community, and now as lead pastor of a center city first church in transition. And one of us (Ken) has helped to plant a new church, has led two flourishing regional churches, and has worked with teams to develop missional communities as a district superintendent and bishop. We were together with a team of twenty-plus visionary leaders who engaged an annual conference in the work of Fresh Expressions. We have learned from our excellent mistakes. And we have witnessed God sightings in new people, new places, and new forms of church.

We are grateful for conversation partners in this journey, among them Martyn Atkins, Graham Cray, Gannon Sims, Chris Backert, Matt Harrell, Kevin Griffin, Elaine Heath, Sue Haupert-Johnson, Jorge Acevedo, Wayne Dickert, Dan Jackson, Janet Earls, Alex Shanks, Cynthia Weems, Jeff-Conklin Miller, Laceye Warner, Greg Jones, Derrick Scott, Jeff St. Clair, Patti Aupperlee, Amy Greene, Robb Webb, Gil Rendle, Janice Huie, Lovett Weems, Kenda Creasy Dean, Roy Terry, Mike Rich, John Boggs, Stephanie Hand, Allen and Deb Hirsch, Vance Rains, Kip Nelson, Robert Schnase, and Ron Robinson.

I (Ken) would like to thank my wife, Pam, as well as the people of the Florida Conference of The United Methodist Church. I (Audrey) would like to thank my husband, José Luis Soto, as well as Branches United Methodist Mission and First United Methodist Church of Miami.

This is a practical theology of ministry for a new form of church. Read it, improve upon it, adapt it, and join in the conversation with us.

WHAT IS A FRESH EXPRESSION?

W hat are Fresh Expressions? By simply hearing the name "Fresh Expressions," some might think it is a laundry detergent and still others a breath freshener. Some who have heard about Fresh Expressions as a movement might interpret it as a last-ditch effort to "save the institutional church." But as we explain in the second part of this chapter, Fresh Expressions isn't another new program but rather a movement of the Holy Spirit.

One of us (Audrey) served in a community that included a large number of immigrant families. Each day many of these men would gather at a central location with the hope of being employed for the day. Many were new to the United States, and most were living day to day. The church began a ministry called Cafe en La Calle. These Monday morning gatherings became as consistent as the Sunday morning services that had happened twenty-four hours earlier. Members of the church, along with the pastor, would prepare coffee and food to share as these men gathered. Individuals could write down prayer requests and put them in a prominently displayed box. At *times, there were deep conversations about family and faith. Cafe en La Calle became a way of sharing the faith in new ways and in a new place among new people.*

1A. A Movement Begins

Do not try to call them back to where they were, and do not try to call them to where you are, as beautiful as that place might seem to you. You must have the courage to go with them to a place that neither you nor they have ever been before.

—Vincent J. Donovan, *Christianity Rediscovered*

We write with a great love for the church but with a sober awareness that the church in the United States is in a fragile place. As leaders within a particular expression of this church (United Methodist), we have experienced the full range of emotions related to this reality: lament, cynicism, denial, critique, and despair. Yet we move forward with the conviction that God is with us.

After two years of strategy, prayer, correspondence, and time set aside in "vision days," we journeyed with friends to England. We went there as students seeking to learn about a movement that God is using to renew the church. This particular movement, Fresh Expressions, has been putting down roots for more than a decade in the United Kingdom and beyond.

The Fresh Expressions movement began in England in 2004 through a report of the Church of England about the state of the church in that nation and the need for a new direction. The report was entitled "Mission Shaped Church." Those who helped to draft the report note that the original title was "Dying to Live," but the early title seemed too dire and inflammatory. The report coincided with the beginning of the ministry of new Archbishop Rowan Williams. In a conversation with Archbishop Rowan, Bishop Graham Cray quickly learned that Williams not only supported Fresh Expressions, but he had also anticipated many of these missional moves in his former archdiocese in Wales.

Upon publication and endorsement of the report by the Church of England, the British Methodist Church immediately became a full partner, through the leadership of Martyn Atkins, General Secretary of the British Methodist Church. Bishop Cray noted that "this [movement] was Anglican and Methodist from day one." Fresh Expressions is an international movement, with partnerships developing in Canada, New Zealand, Australia, and other nations, and across a variety of denominations and theological traditions. Fresh Expressions US is now translating this extraordinary work of God across denominations on American soil.

The phrase "fresh expression" is inspired by the Book of Common Prayer:

> The Church of England…professes the faith uniquely revealed in the Holy Scriptures and set forth in the catholic creeds, which faith the Church is called upon to proclaim afresh in each generation.

Fresh Expressions has a particular purpose for a church or community of faith. Here is the working definition from the Fresh Expressions UK website:

> A fresh expression is a form of church for our changing culture, established primarily for the benefit of people who are not yet members of any church. It will come into being through principles of listening, service, contextual mission and making disciples. It will

have the potential to become a mature expression of church shaped by the gospel and the enduring marks of the church and for its cultural context.

Much of the initial motivation for Fresh Expressions in England was stimulated by the need for new church planting. In the United States, we also continue to invest greatly in new church planting. This work arises from a variety of motives, many of them faithful ones. Meanwhile our cultural landscape is clearly shifting, and we should consider a variety of strategies in response. While the need for new church starts is urgent in the United States, there are cultural and ecclesial shifts afoot that move us toward a new language and a bolder vision.

In a nation increasingly multi-religious and non-religious, many church traditions recognize the need for planting expressions of Christianity outside the pattern of traditional church practice. Careful statistical work by the Church of England and the British Methodist Church documents realities mirrored in the United States. In both Great Britain and the United States, the growth of the unchurched and the dechurched (in other words, the "nones" and the "dones") is rapidly increasing. Some of the "nones" are "openly unchurched" and most of the "dones" fit the pattern of "closed dechurched."

Before encountering the Fresh Expressions movement we thought it was post-denominational, meaning that people of faith no longer prefer denominational systems. However, after listening, worshipping, and observing, Fresh Expressions are better described as deeply ecumenical. Traditions don't lose their distinctiveness. Rather in practice the varied expressions found in a particular tradition contribute the riches of who they are to others, and in return receive new and distinct strengths from beyond themselves. This description differs from the common (and important) work of ecumenical movements, which often occur from the thirty-thousand-foot vantage point of councils, dialogues, and agreements. Fresh Expressions, particularly in post-Christian contexts, will necessarily have a deeply ecumenical character, and yet they will be visible and tangible "on the ground" in a particular mission field. Who knows, possibly this is sign of the in-breaking of the kingdom of God?

In 1989, Stanley Hauerwas and Will Willimon wrote *Resident Aliens,* perhaps the first popular and sustained engagement with the reality that we are now seeking God's kingdom in a post-Christian context in the United States. In some parts of the United States, we see very deep political conflict where some Christians desire a return to Christendom. Our brothers and sisters in England are living more fully in this post-Christian world, and we can learn from their creativity and faithfulness. This is our motivation in partnering with what God is doing through the Holy Spirit in this new venture.

As you engage with these reflections concerning Fresh Expressions of church, we hope you will think and pray about the implications and potential of this movement for your own mission field. The reflections will lead into the study of scripture and together to your call as a disciple, pioneer, and leader.

Bible Study 1

Use this page as a template. Have participants read the chapter before they attend the study or during the study session.

. . . .

Theme: A Movement Begins

. . . .

Prayer: *Ever-present and attentive God, we know that you are with us as we aim to be your church. We pray for open hearts and minds as we learn and study about the ways you are working to make your church fresh for the next generation. Amen.*

. . . .

Scripture Reading: Revelation 2–3
Message to Ephesus
"Write this to the angel of the church in Ephesus:

These are the words of the one who holds the seven stars in his right hand and walks among the seven gold lampstands: I know your works, your labor, and your endurance. I also know that you don't put up with those who are evil. You have tested those who say they are apostles but are not, and you have found them to be liars. You have shown endurance and put up with a lot for my name's sake, and you haven't gotten tired. But I have this against you: you have let go of the love you had at first. So remember the high point from which you have fallen. Change your hearts and lives and do the things you did at first. If you don't, I'm coming to you. I will move your lampstand from its place if you don't change your hearts and lives. But you have this in your favor: you hate what the Nicolaitans are doing, which I also hate. If you can hear, listen to what the Spirit is saying to the churches. I will allow those who emerge victorious to eat from the tree of life, which is in God's paradise.

Message to Smyrna
"Write this to the angel of the church in Smyrna:

These are the words of the one who is the first and the last, who died and came back to life: I know your hardship and poverty (though you are actually rich). I also know the hurtful things that have been spoken about you by those who say they are Jews (though they are not, but are really Satan's synagogue). Don't be afraid of what you are going to suffer. Look! The devil is going to throw some of you into prison in order to test you. You will suffer hardship for ten days. Be faithful even to the point of death, and I will give you the crown of life. If you can hear, listen to what the Spirit is saying to the churches. Those who emerge victorious won't be hurt by the second death.

Message to Pergamum

"Write this to the angel of the church in Pergamum:

These are the words of the one who has the sharp, two-edged sword: I know that you are living right where Satan's throne is. You are holding on to my name, and you didn't break faith with me even at the time that Antipas, my faithful witness, was killed among you, where Satan lives. But I have a few things against you, because you have some there who follow Balaam's teaching. Balaam had taught Balak to trip up the Israelites so that they would eat food sacrificed to idols and commit sexual immorality. In the same way, you have some who follow the Nicolaitans' teaching. So change your hearts and lives. If you don't, I am coming to you soon, and I will make war on them with the sword that comes from my mouth. If you can hear, listen to what the Spirit is saying to the churches. I will give those who emerge victorious some of the hidden manna to eat. I will also give to each of them a white stone with a new name written on it, which no one knows except the one who receives it.

Message to Thyatira

"Write this to the angel of the church in Thyatira:

These are the words of God's Son, whose eyes are like a fiery flame, and whose feet are like fine brass. I know your works, your love and faithfulness, your service and endurance. I also know that the works you have done most recently are even greater than those you did at first. But I have this against you: you put up with that woman, Jezebel, who calls herself a prophet. You allow her to teach and to mislead my servants into committing sexual immorality and eating food sacrificed to idols. I gave her time to change her heart and life, but she refuses to change her life of prostitution. Look! I'm throwing her onto a sickbed. I am casting those who have committed adultery with her into terrible hardship—if they don't change their hearts from following her practices—and I will even put her children to death with disease. Then all the churches will know that I'm the one who examines minds and hearts, and that I will give to each of you what your actions deserve. As for the rest of you in Thyatira—those of you who don't follow this teaching and haven't learned the so-called "deep secrets" of Satan—I won't burden you with anything else. Just hold on to what you have until I come. To those who emerge victorious, keeping my practices until the end, I will give authority over the nations—to rule the nations with an iron rod and smash them like pottery—just as I received authority from my Father. I will also give them the morning star. If you can hear, listen to what the Spirit is saying to the churches.

Message to Sardis

"Write this to the angel of the church in Sardis:

These are the words of the one who holds God's seven spirits and the seven stars: I know your works. You have the reputation of being alive, and you are in fact dead. Wake up and strengthen whatever you have left, teetering on the brink of death, for I've found that your works are far from complete in the eyes of my God. So remember what you received and heard. Hold on to it and change your hearts and lives. If you don't wake up, I will come like a thief, and you won't know what time I will come upon you. But you do have a few people in Sardis who haven't stained their clothing. They will walk with me clothed in white because they are worthy. Those who emerge victorious will wear white clothing like this. I won't scratch out their names from the scroll of life, but will declare their names in the presence of my Father and his angels. If you can hear, listen to what the Spirit is saying to the churches.

Message to Philadelphia

"Write this to the angel of the church in Philadelphia:

These are the words of the one who is holy and true, who has the key of David. Whatever he opens, no one will shut; and whatever he shuts, no one opens. I know your works. Look! I have set in front of you an open door that no one can shut. You have so little power, and yet you have kept my word and haven't denied my name. Because of this I will make the people from Satan's synagogue (who say they are Jews and really aren't, but are lying)—I will make them come and bow down at your feet and realize that I have loved you. Because you kept my command to endure, I will keep you safe through the time of testing that is about to come over the whole world, to test those who live on earth. I'm coming soon. Hold on to what you have so that no one takes your crown. As for those who emerge victorious, I will make them pillars in the temple of my God, and they will never leave it. I will write on them the name of my God and the name of the city of my God, the New Jerusalem that comes down out of heaven from my God. I will also write on them my own new name. If you can hear, listen to what the Spirit is saying to the churches.

Message to Laodicea

"Write this to the angel of the church in Laodicea:

These are the words of the Amen, the faithful and true witness, the ruler of God's creation. I know your works. You are neither cold nor hot. I wish that you were either cold or hot. So because you are lukewarm, and neither hot nor cold, I'm about to spit you out of my mouth. After all, you say, 'I'm rich, and I've grown wealthy, and I don't need a thing.' You don't realize that you are miserable, pathetic, poor, blind, and naked. My advice is that you buy gold from me that has been purified by fire so that you may be rich, and white clothing to wear so that your nakedness won't be shamefully exposed, and ointment to put on your eyes so that you may see. I correct and discipline those whom I love. So be earnest and change your hearts and lives. Look! I'm standing at the door and knocking. If any hear my voice and open the door, I will come in to be with them, and will have dinner with them, and they will have dinner with me. As for those who emerge victorious, I will allow them to sit with me on my throne, just as I emerged victorious and sat down with my Father on his throne. If you can hear, listen to what the Spirit is saying to the churches."

Scripture Reflection

(Suggested answers are in *italics* after the question)

1. What did each church have in common? (*Not too much—they were all different.*)

2. Were the comments about each church positive or negative? (*Both.*)

3. Why did John (*the writer of Revelation*) tell them these things? (*Due to both positive and negative reviews, it seems like John was helping the churches "take stock" of where they were as a church.*)

4. What were some of the positive comments?

5. What were some of the negative comments?

6. Do you notice any of John's commentary applying to what is happening within our church?

7. What do you think John might say to our church today—not to shame the church but to take stock or inventory?

8. Quickly assess your church. Review the missional vital signs (*average worship attendance, weekly giving, number of people weekly serving in the community, number of professions of faith*) of your church and any other statistics the pastor might have for you. As a group consider what these signs communicate about your churches current reality.

. . . .

Transition: *Just as John invited the churches in Revelation to carefully consider their ministries and grow and provide fresh ways of being—spiritually and organizationally—so too Fresh Expressions is offering the same invitation.*

. . . .

Book Reflection: Ask participants the following questions:

1. The origin of the name Fresh Expressions comes from part of the Book of Common Prayer, which states that the church is called to proclaim its faith "afresh in each generation." What does it mean to proclaim our faith "afresh"?

2. This first chapter is full of new vocabulary for most of us. What vocabulary words stood out to you and which one term could you relate to the most? *(If you have not already reviewed the vocabulary list below, you can do so at this point.)*

3. Do you know someone who is a "none" or a "done"?

4. How does the information in this chapter make you feel? Do you feel disheartened? Alone? Helpless? Hopeful?

. . . .

Vocabulary: Each Bible study has a set of vocabulary terms to make sure everyone is speaking the same language and to give people language with which to speak about the church. Review the vocabulary terms with your small group at some point during your session.

-   **Fresh Expression:** A Fresh Expression is a form of church for our changing culture, established primarily for the benefit of people who are not yet members of any church. It will come into being through the practices of listening, service, contextual mission, and making disciples. It will have the potential to become a mature expression of church shaped by the gospel and the enduring marks of the church and for its cultural context.

- **Mission-Shaped Church:** A report commissioned by the Church of England that laid out the foundational principles of Fresh Expressions.

- **Unchurched:** Persons who have never been to church and have no historical or social memory of church.

- **Dechurched:** Persons who did participate in church but no longer participate.

- **Nones:** Persons who do not currently practice a religion.

- **Dones:** Persons who have practiced a religion and no longer observe this practice.

- **Open unchurched:** Persons who have never been to church but are open to going to church.

- **Closed unchurched:** Persons who have never been to church and are closed to the idea of going to church.

- **Denomination:** A branch of the Protestant Christian Church (e.g., United Methodist, Presbyterian).

- **Ecumenical:** A desire for unity and representation among many different denominations.

. . . .

Closing Thought: This Bible study in our congregation is not a task force or a committee but rather a group of people studying together Fresh Expressions and scripture. As you leave today, encourage your group NOT to go home and work on ways to fix the church. RATHER invite them into prayer and more study before you walk together toward solutions.

. . . .

Closing Prayer: *God who has already saved the world, we are grateful that your work does not rest fully on our shoulders. We work with you in your mission. We pray as we continue to guard this information in our*

*hearts that we would have ears to listen to your voice. Guide us we pray
in deeper discernment and study of your church. Amen.*

Additional Questions

1. How do you see the culture changing in your own church and community?

2. What responses seem to connect with persons who are clearly outside the church?

1B. United Methodism and "Saving the Institution"

While current structures are less and less capable of mediating gospel life to increasing numbers of people, we need to resist the temptation of jumping too quickly to proposals for restructuring and reorganizing. Rather, we need to wrestle with questions of theological imagination and discernment such as: How might we go on a journey together of discerning what the Spirit is doing ahead of us in our neighborhoods and communities? How might we join with the Spirit in these places?

—Alan Roxburgh, *Structured for Mission*

Our mission as United Methodists is "to make disciples of Jesus Christ for the transformation of the world." As a United Methodist or Wesleyan expression of Christianity, we are shaped by a few distinctive marks and beliefs about God's grace. We understand these convictions to be deeply held and widely shared core values within the scriptures.

These distinctive marks are (1) the importance of searching the scriptures; (2) the value of singing our faith; (3) the centrality of Holy Communion; (4) relationships of friendship and advocacy with the poor; (5) the necessity of small-group support and accountability; and (6) the power of testimony about the work of God in our lives.

These beliefs are (1) that God's grace is present in our lives prior to our awareness; (2) that the image of God is present in all people; (3) that we are saved by God's grace, through faith and trust, and that this is God's gift, not our achievement; and (4) that salvation is a lifelong process of transformation whereby we love God (personal holiness) and our neighbor (social holiness).

As United Methodists, we are a connectional church. We believe that disciples of Jesus represent him not only in local churches but also in campus ministries, camps, children's homes, immigration ministries, and through missionaries, chaplains, and professors. In this way, the world is our parish: The larger purpose of our becoming disciples is that the world be transformed toward God's purposes and for God's glory.

Increasingly, there is a distinction between discipleship and membership (in a congregation). Discipleship is the more basic, foundational, and essential term for a follower of Jesus. Membership is an important but secondary description of a disciple who is led to give his or her prayers, presence, gifts, service, and witness to strengthen a congregation. Without discipleship, membership can become institutional, perfunctory, and even trivial.

Though a church member can seem to go through the motions, many of us benefit from the existence of institutions. At their best, they embody values that provide our security, health, development, and flourishing. A dynamic relationship transpires between institutions and movements. The Church of England and the British Methodist Church are examples of institutions giving birth to a significant movement—Fresh Expressions.

Given our programmatic orientation in the long-established and declining churches in the United States (including United Methodism), cynicism is a natural response. Some weary church leaders might consider Fresh Expressions to be nothing more than an attempt to "save the church" or "preserve the institution."

We don't attempt to persuade others about their motivations and intentions. We simply share our own experience with leaders and practitioners of the movement in the United Kingdom and the

United States. These expressions seem to be deeply missional with theological convictions that are at the heart of our faith. Leaders and practioners are taking risks to align church structures and channel scarce resources toward a movement that isn't universally affirmed. They have been patient in observing the unfolding work of God that is fruitfulness (John 15).

Some of these leaders have included Rowan Williams, Adrian Chatfield, Graham Cray, Martyn Atkins, Angela Shier-Jones, Bob and Mary Hopkins, Gannon Sims, and Chris Backert. We are impressed by those in leadership roles who are open to innovation and the movement of the Holy Spirit for the sake of God's mission.

An important distinction is apparent between New Church Development (NCD) and Fresh Expressions. Fresh Expressions can be considered one of the pathways God is using to renew the church for the sake of the mission. We will continue to plant new churches through a variety of approaches. Even within New Church Development there is differentiation and creativity, such as multisite campuses or mergers and worship services for particular generational groupings within vital churches.

Fresh Expressions is distinct from New Church Development in that the former will not require an investment in the purchase or renovation of facilities. Fresh Expressions focuses on an investment in people, chiefly by resourcing clergy and lay leaders through coaching, training, supervision, and equipping. Some Fresh Expressions leaders (in the UK they are known as "pioneers") will be bivocational, which means that the best practices of social innovation are crucial. Other pioneers will be clergy who are appointed to contexts that don't require their full-time energy. Gil Rendle noted that in 2008 among the 35,000 congregations in United Methodism in the United States, 10,000 had 35 or fewer in average worship attendance. With this statistic in mind we anticipate that clergy will increasingly live into a "mixed economy" through the direction of their own time and energy toward the mission that is within the walls of the church and the mission that is beyond it. And laity will be authorized to share their gifts in marketplace ministries where many of the next generations live and gather.

In his book *Christian Social Innovation*, Greg Jones speaks to the "maturing" of institutions. Often times we consider maturing as the adaptation of routines, evolution toward something fixed or working toward a set rule of predictability. Yet in his book Dr. Jones points to the work of John W. Gardner who as Secretary of Health, Education, and Welfare led the country in new ways of operating. Gardner wrote,

> Every individual, organization or society must mature, but much depends on how this maturing takes place. A society whose maturing consists simply of acquiring more firmly established ways of doing things is headed for the graveyard—even if it learns to do these things with great and greater skill. In the ever-renewing society what matters is a system or framework within which continuous innovation, renewal and rebirth can occur. (*Self-Renewal*, 5)

In many ways the movement of Fresh Expressions does not aim to save the institution nor eliminate the institution. Rather Fresh Expressions invites the church to continue to mature. The maturing takes place not by settling back into our normal routines of being church and working at doing those better but by stepping out in faith and following the Holy Spirit to new people, in new places and in new ways and in the midst of it finding a renewal and rebirth.

Bible Study 2

Use this page as a template. Feel free to have participants read the chapter before they attend the study or during the study.

....

Theme: The Institution

....

Prayer: *Ever-present and attentive God, we know that you are with us as we aim to be your church. We pray for open hearts and minds as we learn and study about the ways you are working to make your church fresh for the next generation. Amen.*

....

Scripture Reading: Matthew 25:14-30
"The kingdom of heaven is like a man who was leaving on a trip. He called his servants and handed his possessions over to them. To one he gave five valuable coins, and to another he gave two, and to another he gave one. He gave to each servant according to that servant's ability. Then he left on his journey.

"After the man left, the servant who had five valuable coins took them and went to work doing business with them. He gained five more. In the same way, the one who had two valuable coins gained two more. But the servant who had received the one valuable coin dug a hole in the ground and buried his master's money.

"Now after a long time the master of those servants returned and settled accounts with them. The one who had received five valuable coins came forward with five additional coins. He said, 'Master, you gave me five valuable coins. Look, I've gained five more.'

"His master replied, 'Excellent! You are a good and faithful servant! You've been faithful over a little. I'll put you in charge of much. Come, celebrate with me.'

"The second servant also came forward and said, 'Master, you gave me two valuable coins. Look, I've gained two more.'

"His master replied, 'Well done! You are a good and faithful servant. You've been faithful over a little. I'll put you in charge of much. Come, celebrate with me.'

"Now the one who had received one valuable coin came and said, 'Master, I knew that you are a hard man. You harvest grain where you haven't sown. You gather crops where you haven't spread seed. So I was afraid. And I hid my valuable coin in the ground. Here, you have what's yours.'

"His master replied, 'You evil and lazy servant! You knew that I harvest grain where I haven't sown and that I gather crops where I haven't spread seed? In that case, you should have turned my money over to the bankers so that when I returned, you could give me what belonged to me with interest. Therefore, take from him the valuable coin and give it to the one who has ten coins. Those who have much will receive more, and they will have more than they need. But as for those who don't have much, even the little bit they have will be taken away from them. Now take the worthless servant and throw him outside into the darkness.'

"People there will be weeping and grinding their teeth."

Scripture Reflection

(Suggested answers are in *italics* after the question)

1. The parable of the talents is familiar to us! Who can summarize this parable for the group?

2. What was the reasoning, motivation, or feeling behind the last servant burying his talents? *(Fear)*

3. Where did the fear come from? *(He knew the master was harsh and reaped from where he did not sow, basically meaning that the investments he had made were risky and unpredictable.)*

4. Could his fear also come from the fact that he had the smallest number of talents—only one?

5. Clearly the master valued risk. How comfortable are you with risk? What are the advantages and disadvantages of a church who is willing to risk?

Transition: *To truly be the church for the changing culture and religious landscape, the church is going to need to risk. The church might need to lose something in order to gain something greater. Sadly, most churches have taken the third approach as seen in the parable. Thinking they don't have much, most churches have kept what they have the same. The study this week focuses on "the institution," meaning the institution of The United Methodist Church in general as well as the institution that is the local church.*

. . . .

Book Reflection: Ask participants the following questions:

1. What is the mission of The United Methodist Church?

2. What is the difference between discipleship and membership?

3. Do you think Fresh Expressions is meant to "save the church"? What are the ways in which the church needs saving?

4. How might Fresh Expressions be a vehicle that brings more people into a loving relationship with Jesus Christ and their neighbor?

. . . .

Vocabulary: Each Bible study has a set of vocabulary terms to make sure everyone is speaking the same language and to give people language with which to speak about the church. Review the vocabulary terms with your small group at some point during your session.

- **Connectional Church:** A church that is not independent but connected to other churches through a denomination or network of churches.

- **Discipleship:** The process of teaching and mentoring someone in the faith to be a follower of Jesus Christ.

- **Membership:** A promise made by a person to be a member of the church by committing to serve the church through their prayers, presence, gifts, service, and witness.

- **Investment in People:** Rather than investing in buildings or property, investment in people occurs when an organization moves its focus to investing in staff, experiences, and immersion for the people connected to the organization.

- **Social Innovation:** Creating new opportunities, new businesses, and new models to bring about positive social change, often leveraging society itself to bring about those changes.

- **Bi-vocational Ministry:** A person who works in ministry part-time and also works in another vocation; a part-time salary from either vocation would vary by context and contract.

. . . .

Closing Thought: This Bible study is not a task force or a committee but rather a group of people studying together Fresh Expressions and scripture. As you leave today, encourage your group NOT to go home and work on ways to fix the church. RATHER invite them to prayer and more study before you walk together toward solutions.

. . . .

Closing Prayer: *God who risks your own reputation and image through the actions and words of all of us, your people who follow you, we pray that we too might risk. Help us to be comfortable with loss and help us to have new eyes to interpret all forms of gain. Amen.*

Additional Questions

1. How would you briefly summarize the beliefs and practices of United Methodists?

2. How might Fresh Expressions be seen as an attempt to "save" the established churches of the United States?

3. What are the problems and possibilities of bi-vocational ministry?

Citations and Further Reading

Diana Butler Bass, *Christianity for the Rest of Us* (San Francisco: HarperOne, 2006).

Kenneth H. Carter, *A Way of Life in the World: Spiritual Practices for United Methodists* (Nashville: Abingdon, 2004).

Graham Cray, *Mission-Shaped Church: Church Planting and Fresh Expressions of Church in a Changing Context* (London: Church House Publishing, 2009).

J. Gregory Dees, "The Meaning of 'Social Entrepreneurship'," Duke Innovation & Entrepreneurship, May 30, 2001, https://entrepreneurship.duke.edu/news-item/the-meaning-of-social-entrepreneurship/.

Fresh Expressions US, www.freshexpressionsus.org.

Fresh Expressions UK, www.freshexpressions.org.uk.

John W. Gardner, *Self-Renewal* (New York, Norton, 1963).

Stanley Hauerwas and William Willimon, *Resident Aliens* (Nashville: Abingdon, 1989).

Bob and Mary Hopkins, "Streams of Missional Multiplication," http://www.acpi.org.uk/Joomla/index.php?option=com_content&task=view&id=259.

Gregory L. Jones, *Christian Social Innovation* (Nashville: Abingdon, 2016).

Gil Rendle, "The Legacy Conversation: Helping a Congregation Die with Dignity," *Ministry Matters,* February 1, 2011,
http://www.ministrymatters.com/all/entry/716/the-legacy
-conversation-helping-a-congregation-die-with-dignity.

Angela Shier-Jones, *Pioneer Ministry and Fresh Expressions of Church*
(London: SPCK, 2010).

Andrew C. Thompson, *The Means of Grace: Traditioned Practice in
Today's World* (Franklin, TN: Seedbed Publishing, 2015).

Chapter Two

WHY A FRESH EXPRESSION?

Why do we need Fresh Expressions? Many of us ask why we can't stay as we are and just keep praying for better days. The truth is that while we have been working as the church to "change the world," the world has changed around us. In this chapter, we aim to provide insights into how our churches and culture have changed and why Fresh Expressions are needed to respond to this new world.

Patti served as pastor to First Church in Pahokee, Florida, which was an anchor of strength and responsibility for as long as anyone in town could remember. A few miles away, just outside of town, was the state's institution that lodged convicted sex offenders. Patti's shepherding instincts drew her to this community, and she got to know the residents. She discerned that many of the residents had gifts in music and the desire for a worship service. This became the "Church of the Second Chance," and each week the residents gathered to praise God, seek redemption and forgiveness, and listen to the teachings of scripture. The journey has taken Patti and the

*community from listening to the stories of the resi-
dents, seen as outcasts in our culture, to incarnational
presence (simply showing up) to service (offering
and receiving gifts) to making disciples (making time
and space for worship).*

2A. What Kind of Church Will They Inherit?

*Because Christians believe that transformation be-
longs to God, Christian formation—the patterning of
our lives and our communities after Christ's own self-
giving love—requires grace, not determination. The
church's job is to till the soil, prepare the heart, ready
the mind, still the soul, and stay awake so we notice
where God is on the move, and follow.*

—Kenda Creasy Dean, *Almost Christian*

An important distinction in recent reflection about the church is
centered around the words *attractional* and *missional*. An attractional
church sees itself as the center toward which people and resources
flow. A missional church sees itself as a gathering from which people
and resources flow toward the world. Attractional absorbs people
into community. Missional sends them out. And, of course, the most
healthy and vital congregations are both attractional and missional.

The categories of "nones" and "dones" (Pew Research Center,
US) and "unchurched" and "dechurched" (Church Army Research,
UK) make it clear that the renewal of the church won't occur as we
add new and different worship services or develop clever advertising

campaigns (the British call them "schemes") to attract outsiders. Indeed, the conversation about an attractional and missional church is at the heart of the Fresh Expressions movement, although a missional church is not a Fresh Expression, and vice versa.

Fresh Expressions are not attractional, and our experience teaches us that the future is not attractional. Many United Methodists may remember a church advertising campaign with the slogan "open hearts, open minds, open doors." At least in the United States, this openness assumed an attractional church model, in which outsiders would find the insiders to be kind, tolerant, and open-minded people. Upon making this discovery, outsiders would then join us on the inside. Praise God wherever this happened!

However, a significant number of men and women in the United States will never cross the threshold of a church door. This is sometimes due to the actual harm through judgment or neglect that people have experienced from the church. The reluctance also results from perceptions of church in the popular media, where the church and Christians are portrayed in a consistently negative and irrelevant light. Some of our wounds are self-inflicted, and some of the challenge is what George Hunter calls "the end of the home field advantage."

The self-inflicted wounds would be evident from clergy misconduct and boundary violation; exclusion of persons from participation in local churches for reasons that appear hypocritical and judgmental; and acceptance of mediocrity in the teaching and preaching office that renders the gospel as boring and irrelevant. The "end of the home field advantage" signifies that we no longer live in Christendom. In the United States, slightly more than half of the population lives in only 144 counties, while slightly less than half live in the remaining 3,000 counties (according to the research of urban theorist, Richard Florida). In these urban areas, the church is certainly no longer on any kind of "home field."

We find ourselves in the present moment struggling with tectonic shifts in church participation, and there are numerous reasons why. One phrase employed in the Fresh Expressions movement helps to explain how we arrived here: the fragile nature of "inherited church." Inherited church speaks of the orderly process by which a generation passes the faith, wedded to participation in a particular congregation, to the next generation or two. And thus in some churches there are multiple generations of kinship: grandparents, parents, children, and grandchildren. This trend is increasingly not the reality in the Church of England, where 48 percent of the churches include fewer than five persons under the age of 16. This trend is also evident in many United Methodist churches, where in a given year there are no professions or reaffirmations of faith. For example, in 2014 in the Florida Conference, 141 local churches (or 22 percent of congregations) did not have a new faith commitment. Lovett Weems noted that the difference in the rural church of today in the United States, in contrast to thirty years ago is that the rural church is often not multigenerational. If there are no younger people in the rural church, there are not many people to profess their faith and make a commitment to Christ. Graham Cray, in the introduction to *Mission-Shaped Church,* concludes that "the nature of community has so changed that no one strategy will be adequate to fulfill the Anglican incarnational principle" (p. x). The same complexity is apparent in communities throughout the United States.

The inherited church model also assumed that faith was passed along to the next generations in our church in credible ways. Kenda Creasy Dean took a close look at what we are passing along and identified it as "moral therapeutic deism," which is the default theology of many of our youth (and their parents). Moral therapeutic deism is visible in the following propositions:

- A god exists who created and orders the world and watches over life on earth.

- God wants people to be good, nice, and fair to each other, as taught in the Bible and by most world religions.

- The central goal of life is to be happy and to feel good about oneself.

- God is not involved in my life except when I need God to resolve a problem.

- Good people go to heaven when they die.

If subsequent generations don't inherit our church (because of mobility and limitations of where our churches situate in the mission field), and if subsequent generations inherit a faith that is less robust than a generously orthodox, trinitarian, and biblical one, where are we?

Confining our missionary strategy to the traditional parish clearly isn't bearing fruit among denominations and traditions across a wide spectrum of social and political landscapes. The strategic intent of Fresh Expressions lies in its willingness to reclaim the content of faith, to re-center on the movement of the Holy Spirit, and to reimagine church outside the walls of our buildings and beyond the hours of our scheduled services.

As the authors of *Mission-Shaped Church* note, "Perhaps our greatest need is of a baptism of imagination about forms of church" (p. 90). God does indeed go before us, in space and in time, and is not confined by our categories of either/or. For the people called Methodist, this is as simple as rediscovering the power of God's prevenient grace and the call to see the world as our parish. These gifts of divine grace and outward witness are indeed among the most positive characteristics of inheritance, which at times we have neglected, like treasure hidden in a field (Matthew 13).

Bible Study 3

Use this page as a template. Feel free to have participants read this chapter before they attend the study or during the study.

. . . .

Theme: What Kind of Church Will They Inherit?

. . . .

Prayer: *Ever-present and attentive God, we know that you are with us as we aim to be your church. We pray for open hearts and minds as we learn and study about the ways you are working to make your church fresh for the next generation. Amen.*

. . . .

Scripture Reading: Luke 15:11-32

Jesus said, "A certain man had two sons. The younger son said to his father, 'Father, give me my share of the inheritance.' Then the father divided his estate between them. Soon afterward, the younger son gathered everything together and took a trip to a land far away. There, he wasted his wealth through extravagant living.

"When he had used up his resources, a severe food shortage arose in that country and he began to be in need. He hired himself out to one of the citizens of that country, who sent him into his fields to feed pigs. He longed to eat his fill from what the pigs ate, but no one gave him anything. When he came to his senses, he said, 'How many of my father's hired hands have more than enough food, but I'm starving to death! I will get up and go to my father, and say to him, "Father, I have sinned against heaven and against you. I no longer deserve to be called your son. Take me on as one of your hired hands."' So he got up and went to his father.

"While he was still a long way off, his father saw him and was moved with compassion. His father ran to him, hugged him, and kissed him. Then his son said, 'Father, I have sinned against heaven and against you. I no longer deserve to be called your son.' But the father said to his servants, 'Quickly, bring out the best robe and put it on him! Put a ring on his finger and sandals on his feet! Fetch the fattened calf and slaughter it. We must celebrate with feasting because this son of mine was dead and has come back to life! He was lost and is found!' And they began to celebrate.

"Now his older son was in the field. Coming in from the field, he approached the house and heard music and dancing. He called one of the servants and asked what was going on. The servant replied, 'Your brother has arrived, and your father has slaughtered the fattened calf because he received his son back safe and sound.' Then the older son was furious and didn't want to enter in, but his father came out and begged him. He answered his father, 'Look, I've served you all these years, and I never disobeyed your instruction. Yet you've never given me as much as a young goat so I could celebrate with my friends. But when this son of yours returned, after gobbling up your estate on prostitutes, you slaughtered the fattened calf for him.' Then his father said, 'Son, you are always with me, and everything I have is yours. But we had to celebrate and be glad because this brother of yours was dead and is alive. He was lost and is found.'"

Scripture Reflection

(Suggested answers are in *italics* after the question)

1. What does the son ask for in this story? *(His inheritance)*

2. Does the father begrudge him for asking? *(Scripture does not say, although historically we know that asking for inheritance before someone dies would be insulting. Scripture simply says the father divided the land and gave his son what he asked for.)*

3. Does anyone know what the word prodigal means? *(lavishly wasting money, spending money recklessly, wasteful)*

4. In this story the "prodigal son" lives up to his name, wastes his money, and separates himself far from his father. What is the major fault of the son?

5. Do you think it's wrong to want a different life from what your parents had? Live in a city? Live in the country? Have more kids? Have fewer kids?

6. Could it be that the sin of the son was how he spent his inheritance and not so much that he asked for it?

. . . .

Transition: *Luke tells us a story of a son who wants a different life from his dad and so separates himself from his father and wastes everything. In today's churches, our children are not staying around to inherit what we have. Our children want something new. Let's think about what kind of inheritance we are leaving our children.*

. . . .

Book Reflection: Ask participants the following questions:

1. Would you describe our church as a missional church or an attractional church and why?

2. Would you describe our church as an inherited church?

3. As you evaluate our church, what legacy exactly will be bequeathed to the next generation?

4. What type of faith would you like to pass on?

. . . .

Vocabulary: Each Bible study has a set of vocabulary terms to make sure everyone is speaking the same language and to give people language with which to speak about the church. Review the vocabulary terms with your small group at some point during your session.

- **Attractional Church:** A church that sees itself as the center toward which people and resources flow.

- **Missional Church:** A church that sees itself as a gathering from which people and resources flow toward the world.

- **Inherited Church:** The orderly process by which a generation passes the faith, wedded to participation in a particular congregation, to the next generation or two.

· ·

Closing Thought: This Bible study is not a task force or a committee but rather a group of people studying together Fresh Expressions and scripture. As you leave today, encourage your group NOT to go home and work on ways to fix the church. RATHER invite them to prayer and more study before you walk together toward solutions.

· ·

Closing Prayer: *Giver of all good things, you have given us an inheritance in the saving work of your son Jesus Christ. We pray as we continue to be your church we would let go of what is not important and focus on faith as the inheritance we might leave our children.*

Additional Questions

1. In your own congregation, how is the strategy of attractional church working?

2. Do you assume that the next generation will inherit today's church?

2B. The Mission Field That Surrounds Us

A tribe is a group of people connected to one another, connected to a leader, and connected to an idea. For millions of years, human beings have been part of one tribe or another....Human beings can't help it: we need to belong. One of the most powerful of our survival mechanisms is to be a part of a tribe, to contribute to (and take from) a group of like-minded people.

—Seth Godin, *Tribes*

In research from the mid-1990s, a sobering picture of church involvement in the United Kingdom caught the attention of leaders in the Church of England. The following groups were identified:

- Regular attenders: 10%

- Less-regular attenders: 10%

- Unchurched: 40%

- Open Dechurched: 20%

- Closed Dechurched: 20%

The authors of *Mission-Shaped Church* described these as five tribes, each requiring a different missionary approach. They discovered that most evangelism was directed to the nearest 30 percent: less regular attenders and open dechurched persons. This leaves

60 percent of people beyond the mission and vision of the church's witness. There was geographical differentiation; in urban areas, for example, the percentage of unchurched was much higher than 40 percent. However, by 2015, these trends became more pronounced. The passive expectation that vast numbers would "come to us" was a seriously flawed missionary strategy, likened to a "time bomb" (pp. 37–40).

The church in the United States faces a similar urgency. The release of the Pew American Religious Landscape Study in 2016 generated prominent headlines in the general and church media: "Christianity Faces Sharp Decline," the *Washington Post* announced. "America Is Getting Less Christian and Less Religious," according to *Huffington Post*. And in *Christianity Today*, "Evangelicals Stay Strong as Christianity Crumbles."

These and other summaries were shared via social media and became the subject of sermons and lectures for several months. Let's move beyond the headlines and dig more deeply into the data itself. In the United States,

- Christian affiliation is declining as a share of the population.

- Mainline and Catholic churches are experiencing the most significant decline.

- Evangelical and historically black churches are experiencing a slight decline.

- There is small growth in faiths beyond Christianity.

- There is significant growth among the unaffiliated (what Fresh Expressions calls both unchurched and dechurched).

- One-third of the population has a religious identity different from the one in which they were raised (which confirms the decline of the "inherited church").

- Two-thirds of persons who immigrate to the United States are Christians.

- Anglos are more likely to be religiously unaffiliated than blacks or Hispanics.

- Men are more likely to be religiously unaffiliated than women.

We offer three brief interpretations:

First, in most communities, we have clearly moved beyond a culture where persons affiliate with a church as a matter of conformity. A generation ago, it was acceptable and expected that one participated in a church in order to cultivate social, economic, and political relationships. Ed Stetzer distinguished between **cultural, congregational,** and **convictional Christians.** The age of social conformity shaped cultural and congregational Christians, but lacked the capacity to disciple men and women into a convictional and practicing faith. In a survey in 2014 more than five hundred members of The United Methodist Church were asked, "What is the most important issue facing the church today?" The following priorities were identified across the five jurisdictions in the United States:

- Creating disciples of Christ

- Developing spiritual growth in members

- Involving youth (next generations)

- Addressing the decline in membership

These were the four highest-ranked priorities (human sexuality was eighth, and denominational structure was ninth). The responses provide a window into the common experience of many United Methodists: acknowledging the present reality of a church that was built not on discipleship but social conformity, and the future vision of a flourishing church that makes disciples, nurtures spiritual growth, and engages next generations.

Second, the increasing numbers of **"dones"** (those who no longer claim a Christian affiliation, whom the British classify as "dechurched") is the result of two factors. We must first accept responsibility; in the words of the confession, "We have failed to be an obedient church." And so we are honest about the church's self-inflicted wounds, evident in the harm we have done to each other. We should also note that the growth of the unaffiliated has been shaped by the relentless critique of the church both from within (clergy misconduct and congregational conflict) and from without (the high culture of academia and the popular culture of film, television, drama, and music). In social media we are often taken aback by the default posture of cynicism and displaced anger within the church (and among the clergy), which takes the form of self-loathing.

But a third take-away from the data is most significant. The real shifts toward growth of the **"nones"** (an 8 percent increase from 2007–2015) calls us to take seriously movements like Fresh Expressions in the United Kingdom, which is a much more secular context than the United States. One of the core aspects of the Fresh Expressions movement is its focus on emerging networks. In Pew research on Millennials in Adulthood, this generation is described as "detached from institutions, networked with friends." This networking outside the church occurs amidst the varying kinds of millennial experience. David Kinnaman uses the language of "nomads," "prodigals," and "exiles" to describe the diversity of orientations of young adults to Christian community. The fluidity and non-institutional character of Fresh Expressions removes some of the obstacles for emerging generations who are increasingly detached from institutional affiliation. And it is clear that the younger the generation, the lower the figure of participation in Christian community. In other words, it is likely that the next generations will include more nomads, prodigals, and exiles.

One reason for the increase in "nones" is that our evangelism (and pastoral care) is usually practiced among the 30 percent of Christians who are on a continuum somewhere between convictional and congregational faith. We have been preaching to the choir! So how do we engage the 60 percent (inclusive of unchurched and dechurched)? God is calling us to connect with increasingly large numbers of persons outside the church. In each successive generation, church participation becomes less central. And the complexity of our engagement with the mission field is magnified because there is not only one type of person outside the church. Some are unchurched, some dechurched; some are nomads, others prodigals, yet others exiles; some live in neighborhoods surrounding us, and others are more aligned with networks based on affinities.

While sobering, the data is our friend as we seek to "**proclaim the gospel afresh** in each generation." Fresh Expressions, by their very nature, are nimble enough to penetrate the different tribes within the generations and cultures that surround us. The challenge ahead will be the strategic work of making disciples beyond the walls of our churches.

Bible Study 4

Use this page as a template. Feel free to have participants read the chapter before they attend the study or during the study.

. . . .

Theme: The Mission Field That Surrounds Us

. . . .

Prayer: *Ever-present and attentive God, we know that you are with us as we aim to be your church. We pray for open hearts and minds as we learn and study about the ways you are working to make your church fresh for the next generation. Amen.*

. . . .

Scripture Reading: Acts 17:16-34

While Paul waited for them in Athens, he was deeply distressed to find that the city was flooded with idols. He began to interact with the Jews and Gentile God-worshippers in the synagogue. He also addressed whoever happened to be in the marketplace each day. Certain Epicurean and Stoic philosophers engaged him in discussion too. Some said, "What an amateur! What's he trying to say?" Others remarked, "He seems to be a proclaimer of foreign gods." (They said this because he was preaching the good news about Jesus and the resurrection.) They took him into custody and brought him to the council on Mars Hill. "What is this new teaching? Can we learn what you are talking about? You've told us some strange things and we want to know what they mean." (They said this because all Athenians as well as the foreigners who live in Athens used to spend their time doing nothing but talking about or listening to the newest thing.)

Paul stood up in the middle of the council on Mars Hill and said, "People of Athens, I see that you are very religious in every way. As I was walking through town and carefully observing your objects of worship, I even found an altar with this inscription: 'To an unknown God.' What you worship as unknown, I now proclaim to you. God, who made the world and everything in it, is Lord of heaven and earth. He doesn't live in temples made with human hands. Nor is

God served by human hands, as though he needed something, since he is the one who gives life, breath, and everything else. From one person God created every human nation to live on the whole earth, having determined their appointed times and the boundaries of their lands. God made the nations so they would seek him, perhaps even reach out to him and find him. In fact, God isn't far away from any of us. In God we live, move, and exist. As some of your own poets said, 'We are his offspring.'

"Therefore, as God's offspring, we have no need to imagine that the divine being is like a gold, silver, or stone image made by human skill and thought. God overlooks ignorance of these things in times past, but now directs everyone everywhere to change their hearts and lives. This is because God has set a day when he intends to judge the world justly by a man he has appointed. God has given proof of this to everyone by raising him from the dead."

When they heard about the resurrection from the dead, some began to ridicule Paul. However, others said, "We'll hear from you about this again." At that, Paul left the council. Some people joined him and came to believe, including Dionysius, a member of the council on Mars Hill, a woman named Damaris, and several others.

Scripture Reflection

(Suggested answers are in *italics* after the question)

1. Why did Paul begin to talk to the Athenians? *(Because he was there and he noticed their gods.)*

2. Was everyone open to hearing what Paul had to say? *(No.)*

3. What was Paul's reaction to their rejection? *(He kept preaching.)*

4. Did Paul's message change in Acts 17? *(Yes. At first he was very accusatory, but then in verse 22 he begins to reason on their level, relating God to their statue.)*

5. Did all believe Paul's message? *(No, but some did believe and followed him.)*

. . . .

Transition: *In many ways Paul was witnessing to the "closed dechurched." Halfway through his efforts he changed his tone after he saw and felt he wasn't being well received. The data we find in our world today encourages us to creatively find new ways to teach and be with those who are "closed dechurched."*

. . . .

Book Reflection: Ask participants the following questions:

1. What piece of data was most interesting to you?

2. What piece of data makes you feel most uncomfortable?

3. How might you describe someone who is unchurched and someone who is dechurched?

4. Do you know anyone who is unchurched or dechurched?

. . . .

Vocabulary: Each Bible study has a set of vocabulary terms to make sure everyone is speaking the same language and to give people language with which to speak about the church. Review the vocabulary terms with your small group at some point during your session.

- **Nomad:** Someone who travels from church to church without a clear "church home"

- **Prodigal:** Someone who has left the church

- **Exile:** Someone who feels that they have been left out by the church or who has been hurt by the church and thus been forced to leave

. . . .

Closing Thought: This Bible study is not a task force or a committee but rather a group of people studying together Fresh Expressions and scripture. As you leave today, encourage your group NOT to go home and work on ways to fix the church. RATHER invite them to prayer and more study before you walk together toward solutions.

. . . .

Closing Prayer: *God of the nomad, prodigal, and exile, today we pray for the eyes to see and the ears to hear those who are not like us and those who might have something to say that disagrees with us. We pray we would walk close to your heart by showing compassion to all.*

Additional Questions

1. Can you think of an unchurched friend you might characterize as a nomad, prodigal, or exile?

2. Can you differentiate between co-workers who are unchurched and dechurched?

3. How do you live and speak of your faith differently among your co-workers who are unchurched and dechurched?

Citations and Further Reading

Kenneth H. Carter, "Losing the Home Court Advantage," *Huffington Post,* March 8, 2017, http://www.huffingtonpost.com/bishop-ken-carter/losing-the-home-court-adv_b_9377468.html.

Graham Cray, *The Mission-Shaped Church: Church Planting and Fresh Expressions of Church in a Changing Context* (London: Church House Publishing, 2009).

Kenda Creasy Dean, *Almost Christian: What the Faith of Our Teenagers Is Telling the American Church* (New York: Oxford University Press, 2010).

George G. Hunter III, *Should We Change Our Game Plan?* (Nashville: Abingdon, 2013), 12.

David Kinnaman, *You Lost Me* (Grand Rapids: Baker Books, 2011).

Brian McLaren, *The Great Spiritual Migration* (New York: Convergent, 2016).

Pew Research Center, "America's Changing Religious Landscape," May 12, 2015, www.pewforum.org/2015/05/12/americas-changing-religious-landscape/.

Pew Research Center, "Millennials in Adulthood," March 7, 2014, www.pewsocialtrends.org/2014/03/07/millennials-in-adulthood/.

Pew Research Center, "'Nones' on the Rise," October 9, 2012, www.pewforum.org/2012/10/09/nones-on-the-rise/.

Ed Stetzer, "The State of the American Church: Hint: It's Not Dying," *Christianity Today*, October 1, 2013, www.christianity today.com/edstetzer/2013/october/state-of-american-church.html.

United Methodist Committee on Communications, "Membership Poll Data by Jurisdiction," June 1, 2014.

Chapter Three

WHERE ARE THE PEOPLE?

I f people are not in church, where are they? This chapter explores the idea of a "third places." Where is it today that people find community and fellowship if not in the church?

Years ago, one of us (Ken) served a large suburban congregation. When the parents of one of the youth requested an appointment, I wondered what the question might be. It was both simple and complex. The student entering high school was an advanced athlete. He would spend virtually every weekend over the next few years traveling across the United States, learning to develop as a soccer player and being watched and scouted by coaches. "We realize he will miss confirmation and youth. What can we do?" they asked. There were two possible responses. The first was critical: Lay responsibility for the decision in the hands of the family, and then point out the implications of the decision. The second was invitational: Design a small Bible study, held every other week, for the purpose of mentoring the student and other youth in similar situations (e.g., a confirmation class for youth who rotated weekends with blended families). Two pastors and two volunteers took turns leading and mentoring. This was an early awareness that patterns of participation, even among active church members, were shifting.

3A. Where We Actually Live and Gather: An Ordinary Sunday Morning

The connected church of the future will be a church that uses its network of individuals to build new social commons. The connected church will raise up visionaries to see new opportunities for service, for evangelism, and for stewardship.

—C. Andrew Doyle, *Church: A Generous Community Amplified for the Future*

I (Ken) had recently concluded a couple weeks of study and renewal, a time that also included some teaching, meals with students, and conversations with academic leaders. I lived in an extended-stay hotel, which was comfortable, economical, and adjacent to the school where I spent time each day.

On the first Sunday morning, I knew I would attend worship, most likely at 11 a.m. This would give me time to enjoy coffee, read my devotions, and perhaps take a long walk. When I entered the dining area of the hotel, I met a number of the employees who worked at the front desk, in the kitchen area, or as servers. Without exception, all were friendly and welcoming. As I arrived in the dining area, a college field hockey team was just leaving. And then, in a few minutes, another college team from a different school came down for breakfast and filled the room.

I finished my coffee and breakfast, completed my devotions, looked at the calendar, and scanned my iPad. I then went to the front desk and asked if there was an area nearby where I could walk. The desk clerk (who happened to be from Nigeria) was very helpful: "If you cross the street," he said, "you will come into a parking lot of the shopping center. Many people walk there in the mornings and evenings."

And so I looked at the time (I was hoping for a 30–40 minute walk) and stepped outside. I crossed the street and, just as the clerk said, it was fairly quiet and pleasant. I walked about twenty minutes from the hotel, and then began to retrace my steps.

As I walked back, I noticed that the parking lot was beginning to fill up, particularly the spaces nearest the big box store that sold home and building supplies. I noted that seniors, young couples, and single individuals were streaming into the store. And employees were watering plants, putting out signs, and displaying items for sale.

For most of my life, the Sunday morning experience in a local church has been at the center of my experience. This was true in my family of origin, in my young adult years, and in my work as a pastor. A Sunday apart from this rhythm helped me to see three distinct groups of people whose experience is very different. I am not judging them in any way; I simply describe their lives as data that points to the necessity for new and emerging forms of church.

The first grouping included those working on Sunday mornings. We have clearly transitioned from a production economy to an experience economy. People are mobile—they travel to see family (who are also mobile), watch sports, celebrate weddings, and find recreation and renewal. I met people in all of these categories. And there is labor at the heart of serving these persons—lodging, meals, security, housekeeping. My experience in meeting many men and women who work in these fields is that they are quite open to conversations about faith and the church; they are simply in a place where their employment happens at exactly the same time the church traditionally offers worship.

The second grouping included those who are athletes. On this particular morning, both teams in the hotel were female, but they could have been male. Traveling sports begin at an early age, and many young people play a single sport on a year-round basis. Note again the family conversation described earlier in the chapter. "Our son will be playing soccer for the next few years," his mother began, "and we will miss worship more than we will be present. Can we find a different way for him to be confirmed?" Many of these young people play sports in college; many more become lifelong fans who also travel on weekends through the year as adults to watch their favorite teams. Again, they aren't averse to developing in the Christian faith; they are invested in the development of their athletic skills, and committed to the teams on which they play and that they support.

The third grouping consists of men and women who work many hours each week. When they have leisure time (and this is often Sunday), they want to spend that time in their homes or apartments. And because they value these spaces, they want to decorate and improve them. The "do it yourself" industry has exploded both as a form of creativity and as an economic activity. As many spend more time at work and in commuting, there is a pull to stay home on weekends, especially on Sunday. This reality is true in both the United Kingdom and the United States. There was a steady flow of folks entering into that big box department store that Sunday morning; it almost had the feel of some of the large and newer worship centers that have been constructed over the past two decades.

I grew up in a time when there were three television networks. There are now hundreds, and of course movies are now streamed in media beyond the networks. It is interesting that particular televisions networks support and communicate with the second and third groupings: ESPN and HGTV, respectively. These networks can engage these groups with hours of programming and can market products that are appealing to them.

The traditional church doesn't exist in a vacuum. We serve many women and men who can be found in each of these three groups. In the church culture of decades past, we might have been critical of these groupings and their lifestyle choices. We no longer live in a church culture. And yet we as a church have not always been motivated to adapt to a culture whose rhythms of life are shifting. People live and gather in increasingly varied and nontraditional ways. Here I have simply listed three of them.

In the next section we will reflect on how the Fresh Expressions movement addresses our missional context. Going forward, the key learning is that we are shifting from neighborhoods to networks as our primary sources of identity and meaning. And we shouldn't assume that because some people aren't attending our churches, that they are therefore not engaged in a search for God.

Bible Study 5

Use this page as a template. Feel free to have participants read the chapter before they attend the study or during the study.

. . . .

Theme: An Ordinary Sunday Morning

. . . .

Prayer: *Ever-present and attentive God, we know that you are with us as we aim to be your church. We pray for open hearts and minds as we learn and study about the ways you are working to make your church fresh for the next generation. Amen.*

. . . .

Scripture Reading: Romans 12:1-21

So, brothers and sisters, because of God's mercies, I encourage you to present your bodies as a living sacrifice that is holy and pleasing to God. This is your appropriate priestly service. Don't be conformed to the patterns of this world, but be transformed by the renewing of your minds so that you can figure out what God's will is—what is good and pleasing and mature.

Because of the grace that God gave me, I can say to each one of you: don't think of yourself more highly than you ought to think. Instead, be reasonable since God has measured out a portion of faith to each one of you. We have many parts in one body, but the parts don't all have the same function. In the same way, though there are many of us, we are one body in Christ, and individually we belong to each other. We have different gifts that are consistent with God's grace that has been given to us. If your gift is prophecy, you should prophesy in proportion to your faith. If your gift is service, devote yourself to serving. If your gift is teaching, devote yourself to teaching. If your gift is encouragement, devote yourself to encouraging. The one giving should do it with no strings attached. The leader should lead with passion. The one showing mercy should be cheerful.

Love should be shown without pretending. Hate evil, and hold on to what is good. Love each other like the members of your family. Be the best at showing honor to each other. Don't hesitate to be enthusiastic—be on fire in the Spirit as you serve the Lord! Be happy in your hope, stand your ground when you're in trouble, and devote yourselves to prayer. Contribute to the needs of God's people, and welcome strangers into your home. Bless people who harass you— bless and don't curse them. Be happy with those who are happy, and cry with those who are crying. Consider everyone as equal, and don't think that you're better than anyone else. Instead, associate with people who have no status. Don't think that you're so smart. Don't pay back anyone for their evil actions with evil actions, but show respect for what everyone else believes is good.

If possible, to the best of your ability, live at peace with all people. Don't try to get revenge for yourselves, my dear friends, but leave room for God's wrath. It is written, *Revenge belongs to me; I will pay it back, says the Lord. Instead, If your enemy is hungry, feed him; if he is thirsty, give him a drink. By doing this, you will pile burning coals of fire upon his head.* Don't be defeated by evil, but defeat evil with good.

Scripture Reflection

(Suggested answers are in *italics* after the question)

1. What is the spiritual act of worship that Paul describes in Romans? *(Offering your life as a living sacrifice to God.)*

2. What are the patterns of the world that Paul warns Christians not to follow? *(Hating your enemies, wishing bad on someone else, being lazy, etc. See verses 9-13.)*

3. In Romans 13:21, Paul sums up the marks of the Christian life: "Don't be defeated by evil, but defeat evil with good." What are the evils you see in the world today?

. . . .

Transition: *In Romans 12, Paul does not describe the marks of Christians as those who come together and worship at a specific time and place. Our culture has shifted away from Sunday being set aside as a day primarily for worship.*

. . . .

Book Reflection: Ask participants the following questions:

1. What were the three groups the author observes during his Sunday routine away from home? *(The labor force, athletes, and DIYers.)*

2. Are these groups who didn't attend church on Sunday against the church or God? *(We can't know for sure, but it seems that, for many, their decision to work, be on a traveling athletic team, and work on home improvement had nothing to do with how they felt about God.)*

3. What are different ways in which the church might react to these cultural changes? *(Be offended and judgmental; or be open to change.)*

4. How might the church respond to these cultural changes? *(Change worship time, move into the spaces where people are gathering.)*

. . . .

Vocabulary: Each Bible study has a set of vocabulary terms to make sure everyone is speaking the same language and to give people language with which to speak about the church. Review the vocabulary terms with your small group at some point during your session.

- **Networks:** The groupings of people who come together due to interest or hobby.

. . . .

Closing Thought: This Bible study is not a task force or a committee but rather a group of people studying together Fresh Expressions and scripture. As you leave today, encourage your group NOT to go home and work on ways to fix the church. RATHER invite them to prayer and more study before you walk together toward solutions.

. . . .

Closing Prayer: *God who is everywhere, we thank you for your presence in our church buildings but also in all spaces. Today we pray that our hearts might be softened to respond to cultural shifts rather than react in judgment. We thank you for the ways you found each of us and bring us to you. Amen.*

Additional Questions

1. How have patterns of life changed in your own family?

2. How does your congregation respond to Sunday activities in your community?

3B. Where We Actually Live and Gather: Networks and "Third Places"

> The Lord wants us to belong to a Church that knows how to open her arms and welcome everyone, that is not a house for the few, but a house for everyone, where all can be renewed, transformed, sanctified by his love—the strongest and the weakest, sinners, the indifferent, those who feel discouraged or lost.
>
> —Pope Francis, *The Church of Mercy*

One of the key insights in the Fresh Expressions movement is the emergence of the power of networks in the Western world at the beginning of the twenty-first century. As the team writes in *Mission-Shaped Church*, "networks have not replaced neighborhoods, but they change them" (p. 5); and, at the same time, "community is increasingly being reformed around networks" (p. 7). For a personal portrait of this trend, engage again with the content of the previous section, "An Ordinary Sunday Morning," in light of your own experience. Networks are increasingly displacing neighborhoods as our sole sources of community. This is the result of the flow of communication through technology and an increased personal mobility, especially among the young.

A network might center around a hobby (running, hiking, motorcycling, or yoga), around work (information technology, teaching, or health care), or around social justice (activism on behalf of immigrants, the LGBT community, or victims of human trafficking). Members of networks may or may not live in proximity to each other. Their relationships will often be a combination of online communication, either through Twitter and Instagram (younger) or Facebook (midlife or older), and face-to-face meetings. Each kind of meeting reinforces the other, but the pervasiveness of technology allows for a deeper sense of identity that transcends geography or location.

There is much work to do in the formation of community among networks. The challenge of creating and sustaining long-term relationships that are deep and substantive is real. The authors of *Mission-Shaped Church* also comment on the significance of social capital (p. 7) that arises from deep bonds of faithful friendship and community. If we focus solely on neighborhoods, we will miss the reality of communal networks; but if we don't seek to preserve the strengths of neighborhoods (and neighborhood parishes), we won't offer an alternative to the individualization that pervades our culture. This environment is at the heart of the Wesleyan tradition and in our particular understanding of how one grows in grace. Andrew Thompson notes that "social holiness names the environmental context into which Christians are progressively transformed by grace, which is a fundamentally social one," and contrasts it against "solitary holiness," defined as mysticism apart from the concrete community in relation to the world.

This work for community leads to a different contextual question for us: Where is community discovered in our time? The sociological concept of "third places" is helpful in our exploration of neighborhoods and networks. The theory assumes that the two fundamental places where we spend a great deal of our time are home (or apartment) and work. That leads us into the next question: Where does one spend time when not sleeping or working? In Christendom (or church culture), a prominent third place was the nearby church. In the church (say, for example, in the traditional and disappearing Bible Belt of America) one might meet new friends, establish business relationships, play softball or basketball, make political connections, find potential dating relationships, or discover a positive peer group for teenagers. Vestiges of church experiences along these lines do indeed remain, although it is becoming more rare to assume that one will find these in any given congregation. But, if we are honest, this was never the mission of the local house of worship in the first place!

Instead, new third places are emerging in our culture: coffee shops, sporting leagues, digital media, entertainment and resort cultures, and pubs. Next generations such as generation X, millennial, and generation Y especially orient their lives around these third places. Many of us have friends who inhabit coffee shops every day of the week, participate in running groups every weekend without exception, and form community in online relationships on a daily basis.

Sociologist Ray Oldenburg offers insight about the concept of third places. Beyond the social environments of home and work (the first two places), third places are essential for civic engagement and the development of a more inclusive community. He outlines the following as fundamental characteristics of a third place:

- there are no economic barriers to entrance;

- there is food and drink;

- the space is highly accessible;

- there are regulars, who are usually present, and newcomers, who are welcomed and received with ease;

- there is a quality of a neutral space;

- the dominant mode of communication is conversation; and

- the mood is playful.

When summarizing the characteristics of third places, it's apparent that many congregations don't meet a number of these criteria. Our congregations may be composed of middle- or upper-class people; the space may not be accessible; and/or the newcomer experience is often awkward. As churches become more bound to revered traditions (sacred cows), the space can't be neutral; there is a clear distinction between founding families and recent arrivals. For these reasons, the church is called to plant expressions of Christianity in third places that are increasingly "homes away from home" for a mobile and networked society.

It turns out that there is an increasingly large mission field in which to do this creative work. As Jesus said to the disciples, "Open your eyes and notice that the fields are already ripe for the harvest" (John 4:35).

Bible Study 6

Use this page as a template. Feel free to have participants read the chapter before they attend the study or during the study.

. . . .

Theme: Networks and "Third Places"

. . . .

Prayer: *Ever-present and attentive God, we know that you are with us as we aim to be your church. We pray for open hearts and minds as we learn and study about the ways you are working to make your church fresh for the next generation. Amen.*

. . . .

Scripture Reading: Matthew 9:35-38
Jesus traveled among all the cities and villages, teaching in their synagogues, announcing the good news of the kingdom, and healing every disease and every sickness. Now when Jesus saw the crowds, he had compassion for them because they were troubled and helpless, like sheep without a shepherd. Then he said to his disciples, "The size of the harvest is bigger than you can imagine, but there are few workers. Therefore, plead with the Lord of the harvest to send out workers for his harvest."

Scripture Reflection

(Suggested answers are in *italics* after the question)

1. How did Jesus teach and heal and proclaim the good news? *(He went to all the cities and villages.)*

2. When Jesus saw the crowds, he had compassion on them. Why? *(They were harassed and helpless—like sheep without a shepherd.)*

3. Jesus noted that the harvest was plentiful but the workers were few. Would you describe our current climate in the same way?

. . . .

Transition: *Although we might not see the people who are gathering in different places, they are there. In fact, the harvest is plentiful. People are still longing to be healed, taught, and brought into community.*

. . . .

Book Reflection: Read the chapter and ask participants the following questions:

1. What is a third place?

2. What are the third places in your community?

3. What networks are important and meaningful in your life?

4. What is important to your children and grandchildren concerning the world and faith and God?

. . . .

Vocabulary: Each Bible study has a set of vocabulary terms to make sure everyone is speaking the same language and to give people language with which to speak about the church. Review the vocabulary terms with your small group at some point during your session.

- **Social Capital:** Gain to be made within social groups.

- **Third Places:** The space in a person's life where they spend the most time apart from work and home.

- **Social Holiness:** The notion that one's personal holiness is connected to the well-being of other persons, primarily friendships, networks, and communities.

. . . .

Closing Thought: This Bible study is not a task force or a committee but rather a group of people studying together Fresh Expressions and scripture. As you leave today, encourage your group NOT to go home and work on ways to fix the church. RATHER invite them to prayer and more study before you walk together toward solutions.

. . . .

Closing Prayer: *God of the harvest, we see that in fact there is a harvest in our communities. We pray for the courage to seek out third places rather than waiting for people to come to us. Help us to be more like Jesus and go to where people are waiting.*

Additional Questions

1. Can you identify a significant network that is meaningful to you?

2. Can you identify two or three third places that overlap with the neighborhoods where you live and worship?

Citations and Further Reading

Graham Cray, *Mission-Shaped Church: Church Planting and Fresh Expressions of Church in a Changing Context* (London: Church House Publishing, 2009).

C. Andrew Doyle, *Church: A Generous Community Amplified for the Future* (CreateSpace Independent Publishing Platform, 2015).

Ray Oldenburg, *The Great Good Place: Cafés, Coffee Shops, Bookstores, Bars, Hair Salons, and Other Hangouts at the Heart of a Community*, 3rd ed. (New York: Marlowe and Company, 1989).

Andrew Thompson, "From Societies to Society: The Shift from Holiness to Justice in the Wesleyan Tradition," *Methodist Review* 3 (2011): 141–72.

WHEN DO FRESH EXPRESSIONS HAPPEN?

When do Fresh Expressions take place in the life cycle of church? Does a church have to close to have a Fresh Expression? Do Fresh Expressions happen outside of the church? Do Fresh Expressions and traditional churches compete? This chapter aims to explore how Fresh Expressions can begin today and coexist with and even complement the traditional church.

The Nantahala Outdoor Center in the mountains of Western North Carolina attracts canoeists and kayakers from all over the world. The River of Life meets on Sunday morning in an outdoor pub. It is a gathering of locals, millennials, guests, and staff who are seeking a spiritual connection with the natural world. In the weekly time of worship, those present are asked to name "God Moments." This is easier when surrounded by the majesty of the Great Smokies! At the conclusion of the service, those gathered are invited to go down to the stream and touch the water. This moment might also be a call to remember their baptism or seek cleansing and renewal. In recent years, the community has discerned a mission to dig wells that provide clean water in Haiti. In this way, the River of Life is both local and global.

4A. New and Emerging Forms of Church

The dark malaise of the Christian church in our time is that so many congregations have developed a preoccupation with their weaknesses, their problems and their concerns. It is as if there were no open tomb or risen Lord. It is as if these congregations preferred to live locked in a closed tomb, focusing on their past and refusing to recognize the strengths God has shared with them that they might be in mission in this world.

–Kennon Callahan, *Twelve Keys to an Effective Church*

In interpreting the place of Fresh Expressions in the life of the established Church of England, former Archbishop of Canterbury Rowan Williams used the term **"mixed economy of church."** He later regretted this term, although author Graham Cray states that Rowan was inspired in placing the concept at the center of the conversation. In a traditional church, innovation can be perceived as threatening and judgmental. A mixed economy of church includes the traditional and the nontraditional, the cathedral and the pub gathering, fellowship inside the walls of church and beyond it. A "mixed economy" allows for flourishing of what has been and what will be, and is a sign of health.

In an essay in *Faith and Leadership*, Greg Jones reflects on the concept of **traditioned innovation,** which is a pattern of thinking that includes conservation and change. Holding tradition and innovation in tension allows us to avoid "traditionalism," which can result in feelings of being stuck and paralyzing chaos. He writes,

> In our thinking as well as our living, we are oriented toward our end, our *telos*: bearing witness to the reign of God. That is what compels innovation. But our end is also our beginning, because we are called to bear witness to the redemptive work of Christ who is the Word that created the world. We are the carriers of that which has gone before us so we can bear witness faithfully to the future.

We inherit a mixed economy of church values (scripture, tradition, reason, experience), and we journey toward growth through theological values (perfection, entire sanctification, the reign of God, a new heaven and a new earth).

The adaptive challenge, identified by Ronald Heifetz and others, is in part the willingness to "give the work back to the people." For the Christian movement in any context, that gift lies in our locating spiritual practice as close as possible to the experience of the believer, and by extension the gathered community and the surrounding neighborhood. The cycle of Christian history is the transition from movement to institution, or inner awakening to structured preservation. In the New Testament, we see the development, within no more than two generations, from an organic diversity of gifts (1 Corinthians) to a structured ordering of ministry (1 and 2 Timothy). We need both inspiration and coordination, freedom and order.

The question before the mainline churches of the United States, each of them in a state of decline, lies in the challenge of resourcing both tradition and innovation. Can we incorporate experiences of "disruptive innovation" in our lives, or are we more prone to see them as external to us? Most judicatory leaders (superintendents, presbyters, bishops) have encountered resistance in leading change from stakeholders who are already present. This was the Church of England's experience in transition from a missional strategy that was solely parish-based to one that welcomed innovation across parish lines and the planting of new adjacent to existing ministries. The Unites States has also known this type of resistance. A growing sense of urgency is now changing the conversation, especially as splinters form in many established denominations. "In a time of profound missionary need it will be a tragedy if legalism and fear of upsetting clergy prevent creative new initiatives" (*Mission-Shaped Church*, 143).

It is clear to many of us that disruptive innovation (what our friend Jorge Acevedo calls "joining Jesus in his revolution") is the work of the missionary Holy Spirit to which the church is called in the present moment.

One of the ways we experience disruption is in the varied shapes and forms of church participation. These forms range from very large worshipping communities (some even meeting in athletic venues) to microcommunities. These are described in varying ways: megachurches, multisites, new monastic or emergent communities, house churches, Fresh Expressions. The effect they have upon the mainline churches of the United States is profound, and yet, this disruption is not a novel experience.

In the eighteenth century, **John Wesley** sought to renew the Church of England through methodical devotional practices and sacramental experience in parish churches. These devotional practices occurred through a range of experiences: bands (most often four persons of the same gender and a similar spiritual maturity), classes (twelve or so persons, of mixed gender and spiritual maturity), and societies (forty or more persons, who came together to interpret scripture, sing hymns, pray, and share testimony). These differing groups were often led by the laity. The net effect proved to be disruptive to the Church of England, as Methodism ultimately separated from Anglicanism in Great Britain and in the United States. The movement was marked, in the language of Steve Harper, by "waves of grace" that corresponded to the receptivity of growing disciples.

History teaches us that innovative movements become, in time, more structured organizations. This structure can stifle creativity and suppress innovation; the result is that new forms of Christian experience emerge, some developing from within centralized systems— what church historians have called "*ecclesiola in ecclesia*"—and others alongside them. A number of prominent megachurch leaders spent their formative years in traditional denominations; others lead innovative megachurches that do not overtly identify with the denominational label.

Megachurches are innovative in a number of practices: in their concept of theological education (which is more oriented to the laity and more aligned with their own staffing needs); in their succession planning (which in United Methodism is consistent with episcopal consultation and yet has a greater depth and often a longer time horizon); and in their missional engagement (many of these churches have strong staff resources, professional sophistication and accumulated trust, and have assumed the former role of denominational sending or training agencies).

Microcommunities, at the other extreme, are more agile and nimble than the neighborhood church. They aren't invested in property or personnel and can channel their resources and energies toward spiritual practices that appeal to baby boomers, generation x-ers and millennials: prayer and contemplation, face-to-face relationships, and community transformation. Elaine Heath observes that the new monastic and emergent movements share many characteristics in common with the Wesleyan bands, class meetings, and societies of the eighteenth century!

The future will likely be **both/and** rather than **either/or**. And the flourishing of the Christian church will include new and emerging forms that will be shaped less by the institutions of tradition and more by an innovation birthed in mission.

Bible Study 7

Use this page as a template. Feel free to have participants read the chapter before they attend the study or during the study.

. . . .

Theme: New and Emerging Forms of Church

. . . .

Prayer: *Ever-present and attentive God, we know that you are with us as we aim to be your church. We pray for open hearts and minds as we learn and study about the ways you are working to make your church fresh for the next generation. Amen.*

. . . .

Scripture Reading: Acts 11:19-26
Now those who were scattered as a result of the trouble that occurred because of Stephen traveled as far as Phoenicia, Cyprus, and Antioch. They proclaimed the word only to Jews. Among them were some people from Cyprus and Cyrene. They entered Antioch and began to proclaim the good news about the Lord Jesus also to Gentiles. The Lord's power was with them, and a large number came to believe and turned to the Lord.

When the church in Jerusalem heard about this, they sent Barnabas to Antioch. When he arrived and saw evidence of God's grace, he was overjoyed and encouraged everyone to remain fully committed to the Lord. Barnabas responded in this way because he was a good man, whom the Holy Spirit had endowed with exceptional faith. A considerable number of people were added to the Lord. Barnabas went to Tarsus in search of Saul. When he found him, he brought him to Antioch. They were there for a whole year, meeting with the church and teaching large numbers of people. It was in Antioch where the disciples were first labeled "Christians."

Scripture Reflection

(Suggested answers are in *italics* after the question)

1. How did the people from Cyrene and Cyprus get to Antioch? (*They moved there due to fear of persecution.*)

2. In 11:19 we hear that some followers of Jesus were scattered and spoke of the word of God to no one except to Jews. Yet there were a few, such as those from Cyprus and Cyrene, who spoke to Greeks. Why do you think they did this? *(Their faith.)*

3. What was the result of their sharing the word with non-Jews? *(A church was born.)*

4. Up to this point the only place of gathered Christ followers was in Jerusalem. When word got back to the "traditional" church in Jerusalem, what did the church do? *(Send Barnabas as a spy.)*

5. What did Barnabas report? *(Good news, and then he and Saul went and taught for a year in Antioch.)*

6. In Antioch, the spirit of God initiates a new church through laypersons. How else is the church in Antioch new? *(Speaking Greek. In new location. They gave themselves a new name—Christian.)*

. . . .

Transition: *The whole book of Acts is the story of a new church taking shape. Yet, while the new church is in formation, the one in Jerusalem is still lacking. Missionaries from Cyrene and Cyprus went out to new people and proclaimed the gospel. Later they relied on the teaching of Saul and Barnabas. Old and new, order and freedom was used to birth a new church in a new place with new people.*

. . . .

Book Reflection: Ask participants the following questions:

1. In the book of Acts we see that part of forming new communities of faith is leaving our church buildings. If you could leave your church building one Sunday and have church, where would it be?

2. If you could leave your church one Sunday just to meet the people who live around the church, where would you go?

3. How is the culture of the people who live around the church different from the culture of the church?

4. Does your congregation seem open to expressing itself in more than one form?

. . . .

Vocabulary: Each Bible study has a set of vocabulary terms to make sure everyone is speaking the same language and to give people language with which to speak about the church. Review the vocabulary terms with your small group at some point during your session.

- **Mixed Economy of Church:** A church that includes the traditional and nontraditional worship styles, strategies, places, and language.

- **Traditioned Innovation:** A pattern of thinking that includes conservation and change by holding tradition and innovation in tension.

- **Adaptive Challenge:** A willingness to give "work back to the people." Contextually building a spiritual practice with a group of people using their gifts, language, and learning preferences.

. . . .

Closing Thought: This Bible study is not a task force or a committee but rather a group of people studying together about Fresh Expressions and scripture. As you leave today, encourage your group NOT to go home and work on ways to fix the church. RATHER invite them to prayer and more study before you walk together toward solutions.

. . . .

Closing Prayer: *God of all people, especially our neighbors, we pray that we might begin to see those who live around our church. Help us to have the courage of the people from Cyrene and Cyprus who simply spoke to new people to share your gospel. Give us the same abilities to be brave and speak to the people around us. Amen.*

Additional Question

1. Does your congregation seem open to expressing itself in more than one form?

4B. From "Mixed Economy" to "Mixed Ecology" of Church

Israel had forgotten that the vine which the Lord had planted and tended did not exist for itself but in order to give fruit to the Gardener. The gracious indwelling of God with his people is not an invitation to settle down and forget the rest of the world; it is a summons to mission....For Jesus who chose and called them did so not for themselves, alone, but that they should "go and bear fruit."

–Lesslie Newbigin, *The Light Has Come*

In conversation with Martyn Atkins, then General Secretary of the British Methodist Church, he noted that the phrase "mixed economy" (of church) was transitioning to "**mixed ecology**." While the common presence of the word *mixed* allows for diversity of ecclesial forms, an ecological rather than economic metaphor seems more organic and less commercial. At the same time, it also yields itself to conversation with key biblical texts: the laborer in the vineyard (Matthew 20); the sower, the seed, and the soil (Mark 4); the vine and the branches (John 15); and the tree planted by rivers of living water (Psalm 1) are examples of texts that speak of faithfulness and fruitfulness.

These (or comparable) texts could help us rediscover the art of "making disciples for the transformation of the world" (*Book of Discipline*, ¶121). They could be helpful for those persons just beginning to find their way in the Christian life. The passages could be helpful to those who have become dechurched through purging their imaginations of damaging and judgmental stereotypes about God's presence in our lives, and grasping aspects of patience and mercy more fully. And the passages could resource leaders in their catechesis (teaching) in simple and biblical ways. What form the seed takes once it is planted and when it bears fruit is finally the miraculous and creative work of the Master Gardener, and is beyond control. As spiritual guides, we simply search for pathways (John Wesley called them "channels") by which the Holy Spirit yields fruit (Galatians 5).

This distinction is at the heart of *Mission-Shaped Church* and in discussions of new church planting and Fresh Expressions. In an earlier generation of new church development, church plants estimated that they would gather a particular number of participants within a specific time frame; and standardized methods, such as launch activities and mass mailings, were often employed. This often occurred with little regard for cultural or geographic differentiation. Fresh Expressions of church take shape in the environments in which they are undertaken, and they are less likely to be easily categorized. Our task (borrowing from Vincent Donovan's classic *Christianity Rediscovered*) is simply to preach and teach the gospel clearly and faithfully, so that it can be understood and hopefully embraced in every language and culture. We plant, another waters, but God gives the growth (1 Corinthians 3:6).

Gannon Sims, a practitioner for Fresh Expressions US, reminds us that the words *economy* and *ecology* have their roots in the Greek word *oikos*, from which we also get our word *household*. Even as today's culture is in the midst of profound shifts, some related to mobility, migration, technology, and globalization, people are still searching for a sense of place, belonging, and home. The distinction here between neighborhoods and networks, where people sleep and where they actually live, is especially helpful. The institutional church must acknowledge that we have failed to create community in the places where people increasingly live. Instead, we as the institutional church have hoped that lifestyle patterns would in time reverse themselves, and individuals and families would eventually return to predictable patterns of parish allegiance and communal conformity.

Such a return seems unlikely anywhere in the world. In "Be Strong and of Good Courage," Gil Rendle urges us to be "quietly steadfast in the face of nostalgia," which is often the desire to reclaim our past, and to recognize that we are not in a "turnaround situation in which we can recapture the size and strength of a large institutional system once sustained and nourished by a culturally aberrant time." The Fresh Expressions movement is a bold attempt to plant the gospel organically in the **networks** inhabited by the unchurched and dechurched, the "nones," the "dones," and the "spiritual but not religious."

So how is the effort going? Even with more than ten years of substantial investment of resources, it is still too early to draw a conclusion. Here is one report from Bishop Steven Croft of the Sheffield Diocese:

> Over the last 12 years this movement has grown and multiplied and has been resourced in different ways and different places. There are now thousands of fresh expressions of church across every part of the Church of England. Ten dioceses (out of 42) were surveyed for a major study published in 2014. In those dioceses:

> - Fresh Expressions account for 15 percent of churches and 10 percent of attendance

> - In 7 of 10 dioceses, growth of fresh expressions cancels out decline

> - In terms of numbers, these fresh expressions add a further diocese to the Church of England

> - 52 percent of Fresh Expressions are lay led

> - Most are small and growing and part of an existing parish

In the British Methodist Church, 16 percent of reported attendance in October 2013 was found in Fresh Expressions, all of which were less than ten years old. Clearly the church is to be commended for planting new expressions of the gospel in the shifting cultural soil of Great Britain, rather than passively witnessing the decline of participation in traditional forms of church.

Bible Study 8

Use this page as a template. Feel free to have participants read the chapter before they attend the study or during the study.

. . . .

Theme: From "Mixed Economy" to "Mixed Ecology" of Church

. . . .

Prayer: *Ever-present and attentive God, we know that you are with us as we aim to be your church. We pray for open hearts and minds as we learn and study about the ways you are working to make your church fresh for the next generation. Amen.*

. . . .

Scripture Reading: Matthew 13:1-9

That day Jesus went out of the house and sat down beside the lake. Such large crowds gathered around him that he climbed into a boat and sat down. The whole crowd was standing on the shore. He said many things to them in parables: "A farmer went out to scatter seed. As he was scattering seed, some fell on the path, and birds came and ate it. Other seed fell on rocky ground where the soil was shallow. They sprouted immediately because the soil wasn't deep. But when the sun came up, it scorched the plants, and they dried up because they had no roots. Other seed fell among thorny plants. The thorny plants grew and choked them. Other seed fell on good soil and bore fruit, in one case a yield of one hundred to one, in another case a yield of sixty to one, and in another case a yield of thirty to one. Everyone who has ears should pay attention."

Scripture Reflection

(Suggested answers are in *italics* after the question)

1. Do you know any farmers?

2. Can you imagine why farmers might plant seeds in rocky soil?

3. Why didn't the farmer plant in just the good soil? *(We don't know, but maybe this is where we understand the parable in a deeper way?)*

4. In this parable who does the farmer represent? *(Jesus Christ. The Church.)*

5. Could it be that this parable reminds us that our job is to plant?

6. What does this parable teach us about planting the word of God? *(Plant it everywhere—even in the places that might seem "rocky.")*

. . . .

Transition: *This passage calls us to be "foolish farmers" by planting in all types of soil—even those that don't seem like they could produce anything. In the chapter we read this week, we also hear that this is how the church might venture into new church planting.*

. . . .

Book Reflection: Ask participants the following questions:

1. What does it mean to be faithful as a church? *(Faithful to doctrine, faithful to values, faithful to the teachings of Jesus)*

2. What does it mean to be fruitful as a church? *(This might vary from congregation to congregation and denomination. For The United Methodist Church, fruitfulness is often measured by weekly worship attendance, professions of faith, membership, extravagant giving, and weekly service to local community.)*

3. How might a church be faithful and fruitful at the same time?

4. When is it hard to be faithful and fruitful at the same time?

5. How have churches, or your church in particular, failed to be faithful and fruitful at the same time?

6. According to the chapter, what is our task as a church? *(To preach and teach the gospel clearly and faithfully, so that it can be understood and hopefully embraced in every language and culture.)*

· ·

Vocabulary: Each Bible study has a set of vocabulary terms to make sure everyone is speaking the same language and to give people language with which to speak about the church. Review the vocabulary terms with your small group at some point during your session.

- **Mixed Ecology:** An organic model of mixing traditional and modern, inherited and missional.

- **Oikos:** Greek word for house.

· ·

Closing Thought: This Bible study is not a task force or a committee but rather a group of people studying together Fresh Expressions and scripture. As you leave today, encourage your group NOT to go home and work on ways to fix the church. RATHER invite them to prayer and more study before you walk together toward solutions.

· ·

Closing Prayer: *Great farmer, who took a risk on each of us, teach us how to plant in unexpected places. Help us further explore the faith required to reach new people who might be different from us. Amen.*

Additional Questions

1. How would you describe the culture in which your church is planted?

2. Has that culture changed?

3. Has the church adapted its mission to the needs and rhythms of the people who live around your church?

Citations and Further Reading

Martyn Atkins, "Following the Missionary Spirit," *Fresh Expressions*, November 27, 2012, www.freshexpressions.org.uk/missionary spirit/martynatkins.

Kenneth H. Carter, "Generative Christians, Generative Congregations," *The Bishop's Blog*, July 6, 2015, www.flumc.org/blog detail/1500217.

Steven Croft, "Nine Lessons for a Mixed Economy Church," *Diocese of Oxford: Bishop Steven's Blog*, August 25, 2015, www.sheffield .anglican.org/blog/bishop-of-sheffield/archive/nine-lessons -for-a-mixed-economy-church.

Vincent J. Donovan, *Christianity Rediscovered* (Maryknoll, NY: Orbis Books, 2003).

Steve Harper, *The Way to Heaven: The Gospel According to John Wesley*, 2nd ed. (Grand Rapids: Zondervan, 2002).

Elaine Heath and Scott Kisker, *Longing for Spring: A New Vision for Wesleyan Community*, New Monastic Library: Resources for Radical Discipleship (Eugene, OR: Wipf and Stock, 2010).

Ronald Heifetz, Alexander Grashow, and Martin Linsky, *The Practice of Adaptive Leadership: Tools and Tactics for Changing Your Organization and the World* (Cambridge, MA: Harvard Business Press, 2009).

L. Gregory Jones, *Christian Social Innovation: Renewing Wesleyan Witness* (Nashville: Abingdon, 2016).

L. Gregory Jones, "Traditioned Innovation," *Faith and Leadership*, January 29, 2009, www.faithandleadership.com/content /traditioned-innovation.

L. Gregory Jones, Susan Jones, and Kenneth H. Carter, "Mainline Protestants and Disruptive Innovation," *Faith and Leadership*, January 27, 2014, www.faithandleadership.com/features /articles/series-mainline-protestants-and-disruptive-innovation.

The Methodist Church in Britain, "Statistics for Mission," 2014, www.methodist.org.uk/downloads/conf-2014-37-statistics -for-mission.pdf

Gil Rendle, "'Be Strong and of Good Courage': A Call to Quiet Courage in an Anxious Time," August 2016, www.tmf-fdn .org/assets/uploads/docs/Rendle_Courage_monograph.pdf.

Chapter Five

HOW DO FRESH EXPRESSIONS WORK?

ow do Fresh Expressions work? If our mission as a Methodist expression of the church is to make disciples, then how does discipleship happen in a Fresh Expression? Let's explore disciple-making through mentoring and small groups, which is at the heart of the Fresh Expressions movement.

We have a friend who was a very effective clergyman and leader in the church. And yet his most transformational work has always been in one-on-one relationships. Our friend also has a passion for coffee—his passion (addiction?) preceded the wave of artisanal coffee shops across the world. Most mornings you will find him at his favorite coffee shop. While he is an introvert, our friend has found the language to share his faith in natural ways. He knows the baristas, servants, and many of the customers by name. He is frequently reading his Bible and writing in a journal, and he often asks strangers who have become his friends if they would mind if he prayed for them. His presence is a form of mentoring, discipling, and spiritual friendship. He is a model for new kind of missionary, a sign of God's presence within the daily rituals of a culture outside the institutional church.

5A. The Heart of Fresh Expressions: Discipleship as Spiritual Formation and Mentoring

If we are listening to God's call in the present moment, in increasingly unchurched and dechurched environments, we may discover that we are led back to a fundamental experience, which is an encounter with the living Jesus. We encounter him in the Gospels, even as he is anticipated in the Old Testament, and as his message is embodied and proclaimed in the later writings of the New Testament. The encounter is always one that calls us into deeper relationship, which we call discipleship.

Discipleship as Spiritual Formation

How does one become a disciple of Jesus?

Becoming a disciple or apprentice of Jesus is a cumulative process. It involves small steps and giant leaps of faith. It is like swimming against the stream and riding the rapids. It is unconscious and intentional. It is planned and spontaneous. It is work and, at the same time, a gift.

1. As a cumulative process, discipleship is a daily spiritual practice: reading scripture, sending a tweet about a passage

of scripture or a God-sighting, memorizing a verse, offering an intercession, acting with kindness, writing in a journal.

2. Discipleship is also a weekly activity: worshipping God, sharing a meal with a mentor or with friends, reflecting deeply on the neighborhood as a context for mission, encouraging a small group of Facebook friends, contributing money to God's mission.

While the Christian life may begin as an individual search, it can only be sustained and supported through participation in a small group, where we are loved, blessed, and held accountable. The contribution of the Fresh Expressions movement is that these groups aren't confined within our local churches, although they may happen there–this is the "mixed ecology" we spoke of in a previous chapter. And, as we have noted, this is deeply embedded in the practices of the early Wesleyan Christian movement.

---

3. Discipleship as a sustained habit might include monthly experiences: a day of silence and prayer and deeper scripture reading, meeting with a spiritual director, reading a book/spiritual classic, a deeper act of service in the community, serving in a leadership role.

4. And discipleship as a more reflective and long-term way of life might include annual practices: an extended pilgrimage or retreat, a mission trip, or an evaluation of financial giving to God's mission.

5. Discipleship is a lifelong process. In Eugene Peterson's language, it is a "long obedience in the same direction." It will help to document your spiritual formation. For some, there are life-changing events, and for others, the process is more

gradual and even generational. In the Wesleyan tradition, we call this sanctification.

The Bible itself can be read in this way:

- it is the journey of God's people from slavery to freedom;

- the passage of Jesus from baptism and wilderness to suffering, death, and into resurrection;

- the experience of the disciples who follow Jesus, listen to his teaching, witness his death and resurrection, receive the Holy Spirit at Pentecost, and are sent into all the world.

For the unchurched ("nones"), the language of becoming a disciple is entering a new world of practices, habits, and relationships. For the dechurched ("dones"), the path of discipleship requires a detachment from negative experiences of church in the past and a turning toward the gift of new forms of church. And for leaders, lay and clergy, there is the essential and lifelong basic work of spiritual formation. At our best, we will be most effective and faithful as we accompany each other into the future that God is preparing for us.

Making Disciples Through Mentoring

Once we are on the path of being a disciple, we soon discover that we are also called to invite others into this way of life. Thus we need a simple method for making disciples or mentoring friends to be closer followers of Jesus.

So how do we make (or mentor) new disciples?

1. Listen to the other person. This may happen in planned or unplanned ways—a meeting, over a succession of conversations, or perhaps in everyday life. In a culture that is cynical about faith, it is not wise to rush this step. Listening is a lifelong activity!

2. Reflect back to the person who you want to know and understand. For many persons, it is a rare experience to discover that others are listening to and honoring their stories.

These first two steps are essential and cannot be bypassed.

---

3. Connect their story with your own story and a part of the Gospel. This assumes that we know the Gospels (highlighting the importance of daily reading) and can access the presence of Jesus in most any human situation: fear, loss, anger, poverty, betrayal, confusion, pride. You may share an experience where the power of Jesus helped you to overcome an obstacle. This connection isn't about institutions or denominations but is instead about relationships and the spiritual journey.

4. Ask how you can be in prayer for the person, and ask if the other person will pray for you. This places you together on the same level.

Here you will want to be as humble as possible, trusting in the power of the Holy Spirit to speak through the Gospels and the act of prayer. At this point the action is more important than the response, which you can't control.

---

5. Seek to connect the other person to your community. In our time, the basic steps will be a group that meets outside the church (say, in a coffee shop), or in a context of mission and serving, or in a new group in formation. Don't worry if you get stalled here, but don't hesitate to name your own worshipping community. It is a relational process.

6. Stay in touch with the person and continue to develop the relationship—no matter the response. You are investing in the friendship for the sake of the other person and not for any congregational or institutional gain.

7. Continue to pray for the other person each day, and occasionally let the other person know you are doing this.

There is a mutually reinforcing relationship between becoming a disciple (spiritual formation) and making disciples (mentoring). We often learn best by teaching and leading; at the same time, our own lives are shaped, formed, and enriched by deep friendships.

It's also true that where spiritual formation and mentoring are not present, our Christian life can become stagnant and rigid. How do we break this cycle?

If we are stuck, we might seek out a spiritual director, pastor, coach, or guide. This person will be appealing to us not necessarily because of credentials, but more because of his or her authenticity and deep faith.

A word about generations. Many younger adults have a strong need for relationships with persons who are older (not of their generation). At the same time, many younger adults have a great deal to teach older adults. This is sometimes called reverse-mentoring. There is a need for both mentoring and reverse-mentoring in our churches.

By definition, Fresh Expressions "come into being through principles of listening, service, incarnational mission and making disciples." And so our first priority is not to create Fresh Expressions of church; instead, we listen, serve, and become incarnationally present and disciple. In our time, this will take the form of spiritual practices that shape us and intentional relationships that empower others.

Bible Study 9

Use this page as a template. Feel free to have participants read the chapter before they attend the study or during the study.

. . . .

Theme: Discipleship as Spiritual Formation and Mentoring

. . . .

Prayer: *Ever-present and attentive God, we know that you are with us as we aim to be your church. We pray for open hearts and minds as we learn and study about the ways you are working to make your church fresh for the next generation. Amen.*

. . . .

Scripture Reading: Acts 16:1-5

Paul reached Derbe, and then Lystra, where there was a disciple named Timothy. He was the son of a believing Jewish woman and a Greek father. The brothers and sisters in Lystra and Iconium spoke well of him. Paul wanted to take Timothy with him, so he circumcised him. This was because of the Jews who lived in those areas, for they all knew Timothy's father was Greek. As Paul and his companions traveled through the cities, they instructed Gentile believers to keep the regulations put in place by the apostles and elders in Jerusalem. So the churches were strengthened in the faith and every day their numbers flourished.

Scripture Reflection

(Suggested answers are in *italics* after the question)

1. What was Timothy's religious background? *(Faithful Jewish mother, Greek father, and Timothy himself was a disciple and a believer.)*

2. What did other people think about Timothy? *(The community and other believers spoke well of Timothy.)*

3. What did Paul request of Timothy? *(Paul wanted Timothy to accompany him, to be with him along the way.)*

4. What was this mission of Paul and Timothy all about? *(They were delivering news about decisions made by the churches in Jerusalem.)*

. . . .

Transition: *In this chapter of Acts, we notice Paul asked Timothy to accompany him on his trip to visit churches and fill them in on some decisions made by the church in Jerusalem. We do not hear that Timothy preached. We do not hear that he healed. Timothy simply went along with Paul. Paul brought him along to begin the process of mentorship. Mentorship is central to the sustainability of a Fresh Expression as described in the chapter we read this week.*

. . . .

Book Reflection: Ask participants the following questions.

1. What daily, weekly, and monthly practices sustain your faith and walk with God?

2. How would you explain what the Bible is to someone who is unchurched?

3. In this reflection we offer four steps in mentorship: listening, reflecting, connecting one's story, and prayer. Which one of these steps is most natural for you? Which one is more difficult for you?

4. Where have you felt one of these steps most profoundly in your walk?

. . . .

Vocabulary: Each Bible study has a set of vocabulary terms to make sure everyone is speaking the same language and to give people language with which to speak about the church. Review the vocabulary terms with your small group at some point during your session.

- **Cumulative Process:** The process of discipleship the builds over time through study, relationship, worship, and fellowship.

- **Sustainability:** The ability for a church to survive and thrive financially, spiritually, and practically.

- **Reverse-mentoring:** The process of mentoring where the mentor is younger and might be perceived to have less experience or knowledge than the mentee.

. . . .

Closing Thought: This Bible study is not a task force or a committee but rather a group of people studying together Fresh Expressions and scripture. As you leave today, encourage your group NOT to go home and work on ways to fix the church. RATHER invite them to prayer and more study before you walk together toward solutions.

. . . .

Closing Prayer: *God who came to mentor twelve disciples, you call us to be in the work of mentorship. We pray that you would enlighten us to whom you are calling to do the work of your people in our community. Lead us and direct us and rise up leaders within our church. Amen.*

Additional Questions

1. What two or three spiritual practices or habits would strengthen your life as a disciple of Jesus?

2. What happens weekly, or monthly, or annually?

3. Is there someone in your network or community who might be open to your spiritual mentoring?

5B. Sustaining Fresh Expressions: A Deeper Dive into Discipleship

---

Methodism was a holiness movement that initiated people into a holy life, revealed in Jesus Christ, anchored in the church, empowered by the Holy Spirit, surrendered to the reign of God, for the transformation of the world.

—Elaine Heath and Scott Kisker, *Longing for Spring*

The Wesleyan movement began as a "method" of making disciples. Kevin Watson locates the essential shape of Wesleyan discipleship in the small group, which focused on "the free inquiry into the state of the heart" (Francis Asbury, quoted in *The Class Meeting*, 30). In groups small enough to know and be known, men and women were willing to leave the old life behind (**class meeting**) and make progress together in holiness (**band meeting**). In these relationships, individuals "watched over one another in love" through support and accountability.

As Steve Harper notes in *The Way to Heaven*, the early Methodist movement was "thoroughly ecumenical in character." No one had to leave his or her church in order to be a Methodist. For much of his life, Wesley saw to it that the Methodist meetings didn't conflict with the worship hours of the churches (p. 123). Many of our questions related to the emergence of Fresh Expressions are shaped by existing forms of church; the early Wesleyan movement developed alongside the predominant patterns of church, taking up the essential work alongside them.

If we are to "make disciples of Jesus Christ for the transformation of the world" (*Book of Discipline*, ¶121), we will rediscover the DNA in our own tradition and learn from leaders and practitioners of renewal movements in our own day. Mike Breen, co-author of *Building a Discipleship Culture*, speaks of discipleship as information, imitation, and immersion. We shouldn't conceive of disciple-making as being exclusive to any one of these actions, for "if you make disciples, you will always get the church. But if you try to build the church, you will rarely get disciples."

So how are disciples being made in our own time and place? Most United Methodists are exposed to sufficient **information**: texts, curriculum, and sermon series, among others. These are valuable resources, and God uses them to teach us. Many Christians are formed through high-commitment Bible studies offered in congregations. Increasingly, the worship service itself is the setting for adult formation, particularly through the use of sermon series. These are highly visible examples of information and, in an increasing biblically illiterate culture, information is necessary. Anecdotal evidence suggests that many men and women attend seminaries in order to be exposed, for the first time, to basic teaching about scripture, church history, and doctrine.

Imitation is murky in the present United Methodist experience. We are more committed to the reception of information than to the practice of imitation, where we learn from a role model who invests time in us. Yet many of us have been blessed by mentors along the way. The loss of the class meeting separated us from the model of the class leader. Many imitate the clergy leader by discerning a call to be set apart in ministry of some sort. In a highly committee-based structure, there is much apprenticeship in what Ken Callahan called the "functional" areas of ministry, so the incoming trustee chair might shadow the present chair. It may be that we are stronger in discipling leaders for the administration of the church than in the more foundational areas of prayer, scripture reading, service, and justice ministries. Or at least these latter ministries are perhaps more hidden and contextual.

Through **immersion** we make connections between the information we have received and the role models we have watched, and we discover ourselves to be in environments that are transformational. Immersion has happened chiefly in outdoor ministries such as camps, short-term mission teams, and in the Walk to Emmaus retreats. It is emerging in forms of new monasticism and in the work (theory and practice) of Elaine Heath. For many, immersion happens as students are formed (liturgically, intellectually, communally) in theological schools.

This reflection on discipleship is somewhat institutional and theoretical, so let's consider something more fundamental, constructive, and helpful to practitioners—participants in Fresh Expressions and the spiritual guides of these communities. When the traditional elements of parish, church, and neighborhood are stripped away, as they have become for so many, and when the primary context is a network or a third place, we are forced (and perhaps this is good) to clarify what it means to become a disciple of Jesus and to make disciples of others.

In a poll taken of clergy and laity members of The United Methodist Church in June 2014, the two most important priorities were "creating disciples of Christ" and "the spiritual growth of members." The next two were "youth involvement" and "decline in membership." We are often focused on other priorities in the life of the church, but this data reminds us to ask: How do we become disciples, and how do we make disciples? These are fundamental questions at the heart of the Fresh Expressions movement and the flourishing of the church.

Bible Study 10

Use this page as a template. Feel free to have participants read the chapter before they attend the study or during the study.

. . . .

Theme: A Deeper Dive into Discipleship

. . . .

Prayer: *Ever-present and attentive God, we know that you are with us as we aim to be your church. We pray for open hearts and minds as we learn and study about the ways you are working to make your church fresh for the next generation. Amen.*

. . . .

Scripture Reading: Acts 6:1-7

About that time, while the number of disciples continued to increase, a complaint arose. Greek-speaking disciples accused the Aramaic-speaking disciples because their widows were being overlooked in the daily food service. The Twelve called a meeting of all the disciples and said, "It isn't right for us to set aside proclamation of God's word in order to serve tables. Brothers and sisters, carefully choose seven well-respected men from among you. They must be well-respected and endowed by the Spirit with exceptional wisdom. We will put them in charge of this concern. As for us, we will devote ourselves to prayer and the service of proclaiming the word." This proposal pleased the entire community. They selected Stephen, a man endowed by the Holy Spirit with exceptional faith, Philip, Prochorus, Nicanor, Timon, Parmenas, and Nicolaus from Antioch, a convert to Judaism. The community presented these seven to the apostles, who prayed and laid their hands on them. God's word continued to grow. The number of disciples in Jerusalem increased significantly. Even a large group of priests embraced the faith.

Scripture Reflection

(Suggested answers are in *italics* after the question)

1. What was the complaint brought against the disciples?
   (The widows were being overlooked during the daily food distribution.)

2. What was the disciples' response? *(We can't give up on reading the word to wait tables.)*

3. Did the disciples completely give up their missional task with the widows? *(No.)*

4. Instead how did they solve the problem? *(They created more disciples.)*

5. What was the result of their decision? *(Everyone was content and the making of more disciples took place.)*

. . . .

Transition: *In the book of Acts, in order for the movement to keep going, the twelve disciples realized they could not do it all. So instead they appointed new disciples. This caused the formation of even more disciples. This scripture also brings to light that the work of the disciple is both missional and spiritual. For Fresh Expressions to be formed and sustained, discipleship is key.*

. . . .

Book Reflection: Ask participants the following questions:

1. When is the last time someone asked you, "How is it with your heart?"

2. This question above was at the center of Wesley's discipleship method. How does this relate to other groups you are currently part of in the congregation?

3. In this chapter we learn that discipleship happens in three ways: information, imitation, and immersion. Where can you see these methods taking place in your congregation?

4. Who "discipled" you to be in a deeper relationship with Jesus Christ?

. . . .

Vocabulary: Each Bible study has a set of vocabulary terms to make sure everyone is speaking the same language and to give people language with which to speak about the church. Review the vocabulary terms with your small group at some point during your session.

- **Class Meeting:** The Wesleyan introductory meeting of people gathering together to share life's journey of work, home, and faith with each other.

- **Band Meeting:** The Wesleyan meeting of people who provide accountability to one another regarding study, tithing, mission, participation, and worship.

. . . .

Closing Thought: This Bible study is not a task force or a committee but rather a group of people studying together Fresh Expressions and scripture. As you leave today, encourage your group NOT to go home and work on ways to fix the church. RATHER invite them to prayer and more study before you walk together toward solutions.

. . . .

Closing Prayer: *God who calls us to each other, we pray today that you would grow within us the desire to be together. Grow within us the desire to teach about you. Grow within us a desire to imitate you and be immersed in you. Bind us together by your Holy Spirit. Amen.*

Additional Questions

1. Where would one likely find accountability and support in your congregation?

2. Can you recall powerful experiences of information, imitation, and immersion in your own journey?

Citations and Further Reading

William J. Abraham, *The Logic of Evangelism* (Grand Rapids: Eerdmans, 1989).

Mike Breen, "Why the Missional Movement Will Fail," Verge Network, accessed March 30, 2017, http://www.vergenetwork.org/2011/09/14/mike-breen-why-the-missional-movement-will-fail/.

Mike Breen and the 3DM Team, *Building a Discipleship Culture*, 2nd ed. (Pawleys Island, SC: 3DM Publishing, 2014).

Kennon Callahan, *Twelve Keys to an Effective Church: Strong, Healthy Congregations Living in the Grace of God*, 2nd ed. (San Francisco: Jossey-Bass, 2010).

Samuel G. Freedman, "Secular, But Feeling a Call to Divinity School," *New York Times*, October 16, 2015, www.nytimes.com/2015/10/17/us/more-students-secular-but-feeling-a-call-turn-to-divinity-schools.html?_r=0.

Steve Harper, *The Way to Heaven: The Gospel According to John Wesley*, 2nd ed. (Grand Rapids: Zondervan, 2002).

"How Do You Define a Fresh Expression of Church?" *Fresh Expressions*, www.freshexpressions.org.uk/ask/define.

Kenneth Leech, *Soul Friend*, rev. ed. (New York: Morehouse Publishing, 2001).

Eugene Peterson, *A Long Obedience in the Same Direction: Discipleship in an Instant Society,* 20th anniv. ed. (Downers Grove, IL: IVP Books, 2000).

Kevin Watson, *The Class Meeting: Reclaiming a Forgotten (and Essential) Small Group Experience* (Franklin, TN: Seedbed Publishing, 2013).

WHO STARTS FRESH EXPRESSIONS?

Who can start a Fresh Expression? Some might have heard that Fresh Expressions are only for millennials, but actually the Holy Spirit is the start of every Fresh Expression, and the Holy Spirit uses the gifts and grace of everyone. Every person in the congregation and in the institutional church has an important role to play in the creation of Fresh Expressions. This chapter aims to point toward the work of the Holy Spirit before us and the importance of each role in a Fresh Expression.

Our brothers and sisters in the Methodist Church of Cuba have found a way to thrive. Brian McLaren once commented that two of the most hopeful signs of Christianity's flourishing across the planet were the Fresh Expressions movement in England and the church in Cuba. In Cuba, a leader feels called to form a community, and the first fruits of that is a cell group. In time, if there is growth, the community begins to look more like a house church. There is singing and worship, testimony, and a shared meal. And, with more time, the house church may grow to become a church, located in a building. The progression is organic, and leadership emerges within and is blessed by the community. When the community becomes a church, the spiritual leader is ordained. There is just enough structure to support the mission. So which comes first: the Holy Spirit or the church?

6A. Where Are You in the Movement? The Fresh Expressions Village

The Fresh Expressions movement includes several varied and distinct persons who contribute to the whole. Not all have the same gifts and callings (1 Corinthians 12), and yet the body of Christ is strengthened by this diversity; indeed, this is the complex and beautiful pattern of ministry in the New Testament.

A fresh expression of church will by design not be the work of one heroic solo leader; instead, as the phrase goes, it will take a village to create and sustain a growing and healthy community of men and women who are listening to each other, offering themselves in service, engaging in incarnational mission, and making disciples of Jesus Christ.

This village will include the following persons:

Practitioners: The people who do the work of listening, loving, serving, creating community, forming worship, and making disciples are **practitioners** of Fresh Expressions. Practitioner or "pioneers," as Fresh Expressions UK calls them, are both lay and clergy who are missionaries at heart. Practitioners are people who model the example of Christ described by Paul in Philippians 2. Lay and clergy practitioners immerse themselves in a new community. Their aim is to listen to a new culture and serve the new community rather than tell them how to be church and impose their own culture on the community. It was no surprise to learn that the vast majority of pioneers with Fresh Expressions UK were former missionaries or children of missionaries. Many pioneers learned new languages and cultures when living in other countries and are now applying their lifestyle as missionaries abroad to fulfill their call in forming fresh expressions of church.

Many of the pioneers in England are laypersons. We find that many laypeople want to reach new people and get beyond their walls, but do not know how to do it. We have also found that many laypeople are gifted in evangelism and discipleship. In The United Methodist Church, the Disciple Bible Study series, followed by Covenant Bible Study, created a culture of very learned laypersons. In Fresh Expressions Florida, our goal was to have 50 percent of lay participation in all of our trainings, and we have currently made that goal. As lay and clergy engage in Fresh Expressions, it's important to remember that Fresh Expressions doesn't change *what* we are doing but rather *how* we are doing it. Fresh Expressions teach, evangelize, transform, and empower people to be Christ-followers much like the traditional church and the ancient church. Yet the *way* in which we go about this work looks very different.

Practitioners are people who work toward testing, trying, and implementing new ways of being church with new people and in new places. Practitioners will most likely be risk-takers and those who learn fast from failures and keep working in order to succeed sooner. The risk might be placing oneself in an unfamiliar community that speaks a different language. The failure in that situation might be unintentionally saying something offensive. Practitioners are those who will apologize, learn from their mistakes, and seek the help of the community. As one could imagine, the role of the practitioner is important but can also at times be frustrating, and it's a role that needs continued support. For this, a missional mentor is essential.

Missional Mentors: In their book *Coaching for Missional Leadership,* Bob Hopkins and Freddy Hedley distinguish between task-centered consultants and person-centered mentors. A calling-centered coach, in their framework, combines both of these activities in a somewhat balanced process. For our purposes, we are using the term *missional mentors.* Missional mentors attend to the needs of the mission and the leader and use the tools of spiritual direction, coaching, consulting, missiology, evangelism, and their own personal experience.

Life in a mission field can be chaotic. Unpredictability is the norm. Neatly defined rules, regulations, and procedures don't square with our experience. Visible fruit is often difficult to assess. Pioneers travel alone at their peril. There is often a sense of isolation and, at times, despair. We are deeply into the transition from a church culture to a mission field. On a mission field, there's a need for help. There are a number of roles that have emerged in the church to describe the exact nature of the help needed: spiritual direction, coaching, guiding, and supervision.

The missional mentor will draw upon the coaching practice of asking questions, drawing upon the strengths of the pioneer, and walking alongside. He or she will be a hopeful and encouraging presence, drawing upon the authority of experience, shared wisdom, and at times their position in the church, while being intentionally aware that the focus is on the pioneer leader.

Interpreters: There is an ongoing need in the development of Fresh Expressions to interpret what this movement means. The presence of something new (fresh!) can create worry and apprehension.

Some leaders or persons in authority will wonder if they are being displaced. Others will question the validity of the form or substance of Fresh Expressions. And yet others will simply define the present status quo, in which they may be already heavily invested, as a Fresh Expression of church.

For these reasons the movement depends upon the skillful interpretation of what is happening. This interpretation will include listening and speaking. The listening may alleviate the anxieties, fears, and misunderstandings. Skillful speaking will invite people into the movement. Martyn Atkins often begins a conversation by asking, "Would you be willing to create a church that your grandchildren would love?" The interpretation of the relationship of the traditional church and fresh expressions is key to the role of Fresh Expressions. A strength of the movement is the critical concept of "mixed economy" of church, which honors the needs and experiences of multiple generations (for example, the grandparent and the grandchild); in the Missional Wisdom movement led by Elaine Heath, there is the crucial role of the anchor church, and in the United Kingdom, many of the cathedrals are thriving. There is a need for traditional forms of church, and yet God is also calling us into a movement that is innovative, fresh, and generative.

Much of the interpretation may take the form of telling stories of how lives are transformed and how community is discovered. As we have noted, interpretation will include connecting this movement beyond the walls of the church.

Rowan Williams, the former Archbishop of Canterbury, posed a question voiced by many: "Is it really church?" He writes,

> The "strength" of the Church is never anything other than the strength of the presence of the Risen Jesus. And one thing this means is that, once we are convinced that God in Jesus Christ is indeed committed to us and present with us, there is a certain freedom to risk everything except those things that hold us to the truth

of his presence—Word and sacrament and the journey into holiness. These will survive, whatever happens to this or that style of worship, this or that bit of local Christian culture, because the presence of Jesus in the community will survive.

Here is a masterful example of interpretation, and, given Williams's role, a model of permission-giving as well.

Stewards: The Fresh Expressions movement will require resources that are invested not so much in property as in people. Our growing conviction is that we will need to rediscover healthy and intentional financial practices if we are to support and sustain vital witness in the years ahead. The steward will integrate the gifts of at least two kinds of persons, the patron and the tentmaker. The patron is someone with means who is inspired to fund a cause. It is clear that Jesus traveled with patrons, often women, who helped to support his ministry. Those who lead Christian institutions are well aware of the impact of an infusion of resources: an innovative initiative can begin, a neglected area of ministry can be served, a new population can be reached.

In the past generation, Lilly Endowment Inc., The Duke Endowment, the Texas Methodist Foundation, and others have made significant contributions toward theological education and lifelong formation of clergy. Most congregational and judicatory leaders over time develop relationships with patrons who make significant mission possible. While the typical pastor has little training in development, along the way the skill of cultivating patrons becomes as integral to the practice of effective ministry as preaching, teaching, and shepherding.

There are, however, some weaknesses in the patron model: the leader or organization can become dependent on an individual or an endowment; over time, the actual mission can become distant from the original intent of the donor; and the presence of an influential patron can have a flattening effect on the participation of persons at the grassroots level.

In his letters to the earliest churches, Paul clearly states at times that he is supporting himself and taking no funds from the actual congregations. In the New Testament we find a model for ministry that is bi-vocational: at times the leader is supported by the congregation, and at times he or she is sustained by some other livelihood. This is the tentmaker.

A great strength of the tentmaker model is purity of motive. Paul writes that he is doing the mission for its own sake and not for personal gain. We think that the bi-vocational model is one that the mainline churches of the United States will increasingly embrace. In our own tradition, United Methodism, more than one-third of our local churches in the United States have fewer than thirty-five persons in worship on a given Sunday. These communities are often vital expressions of fellowship and service in their contexts; at the same time, they cannot sustain full-time clergy leadership.

An additional strength of bi-vocational ministry is its stability. As a pastor develops a business or assumes an additional professional role in the community, he or she is more rooted there and is able to give smaller congregations continuity.

The churches of the New Testament flourished in a disorderly, chaotic, and missional environment. In contrast, the mainline churches of the United States have depended, for more than a generation, on a predictable stream of revenue that flowed from individuals shaped by a church culture.

We find ourselves now in a culture more closely aligned with the first-century communities where the earliest churches and missions were planted. A changed context calls for a fresh exploration of models for funding ministry.

Rediscovering the ancient-future practices of a missional movement, and re-imagining the roles of patron and tentmaker in our own time, may help us to support the renewal of our congregations and sustainability of Fresh Expressions.

Permission-Givers: People in our churches are ready to do new things in the church. More and more seminary students and young people who have been formed by thriving campus ministries have expressed their great need and desire to be part of Fresh Expressions. So what is holding them back? The answer is simple: permission. There are some who do not sense a need to ask for permission (from clergy supervisors or lay leaders); they simply move forward in the creation of a Fresh Expression. Yet, the majority of pastors and laypersons fear rejection, failure, ridicule, and possible termination from their roles and positions. Permission-givers are as equal an ingredient as a practitioner in the recipe that comes together to form a Fresh Expression. Without permission-givers, practitioners might not even begin to dream or pray about a fresh expression.

We each attended a divinity school known for its university basketball team. And so we have played with an analogy from basketball that helps to sketch the role that permission-givers can play in Fresh Expressions.

- Bishops can be compared to the coach of the team. The episcopal leader casts the vision and identifies players and leaders. On the mission field, permission-givers cast a vision for new ways of being church.

- Missional mentors are the assistant coaches who help the team run the plays and find a path forward. They work alongside the players in practice and identify strengths and weakness, giving encouragement and making corrections.

- District superintendents play the role of a screening forward, strategically anticipating where there might be resistance and working to protect and empower the practitioners, who might be classified as the point guard. Superintendents can also function creatively as missional mentors.

- At the congregational level, existing members might not be pioneers, but they are still players. A trustee chair or church council member might be a forward who comes alongside the guard, whose action begins the play. Laity might literally give permission by making the decision to use an old parsonage as a community center for a home church. They give permission by guiding and directing church energies and resources toward Fresh Expressions. The staff parish relations committee might give permission by giving the pastor the freedom to spend five hours or ten hours a week developing a Fresh Expression in the neighborhood. And there are also encouragers, in the stands cheering us on!

The basketball analogy also works well in that it creates the understanding that there will be an ebb and flow to the work of a Fresh Expression. There will bursts of energy and momentum—fast breaks—and then the action will seem to move very slowly—as if someone is running out the clock! As we practice, our skills and talents will improve, and we will discover the strengths that reside in each other. Most certainly there will also be victories for God's reign. And we cannot forget that in every great basketball game there are commercials; these remind us of the crucial need for material support by God's people that sustains all of the action, and for the role of the steward!

Prayer Partners: "Fresh Expressions is not for me. I don't get it." These were the words of one participant during a Spark Day we hosted. The woman stated her feelings honestly about Fresh Expressions. Believe it or not, she was not the first to voice these feelings about Fresh Expressions. There will be many who don't "get it" and don't want to be part of the work of Fresh Expressions, which is perfectly okay! But after much conversation, we found that although she did not get Fresh Expressions she did get prayer. She left the engagement committing to pray for her pastor and for the people in her community each day. Although some don't want to be part of the work, they can be part of the praying! Prayer is essential to the work of Fresh Expressions. If we are to be guided by the Holy Spirit, prayer is a vehicle by which to listen. Fresh Expressions thrive most when they are built alongside a team of faithful prayer partners. Prayer partners can be members of a church launching a Fresh Expression or simply friends and neighbors who believe in the work and want to pray for it.

Collaborators: Institutionally and externally, Fresh Expressions can't exist without collaborators. Institutionally, collaborators might be found in a new church development office or a church vitality team. The work of Fresh Expressions and new church planting is not competitive but very much complementary. In the Florida Conference of The United Methodist Church, the office of New Church Development and Vitality allocated part of their budget to get Fresh Expressions started within our conference. The directors of the offices sit on the steering committee and are integral parts of connecting the work of Fresh Expressions with the churches in the conference.

Person of Peace: Externally, Fresh Expressions will aim to find a "person of peace." A person of peace is someone who is part of the culture or community you feel called to reach. This person is not resistant to the presence of a practitioner but rather the practitioner has formed an authentic relationship of trust with this person. The person is then able to connect the work of the individual Fresh Expression with people and resources within that community.

For example, First United Methodist Church of Miami began Yoga Chapel that incorporates prayer, scripture, devotion, service, and giving into a weekly hour-long yoga class. Our person of peace had a relationship with the church, although he wasn't a member. This person is the church's soloist and also a student at a nearby college. Our paid soloist loved yoga and quickly became one of our best volunteers and recruiters. In over a year, our person of peace became an evangelist and inviter and also brought a new teacher to Yoga Chapel. The people he invited had not been to church since experiencing first communion in their home countries. Most of the participants in the group were suspicious of "the church," but had a great openness to spirituality. They might be categorized as open de-churched. Our person of peace was integral in bringing new people to be part of Yoga Chapel.

Bible Study 11

Use this page as a template. Feel free to have participants read the chapter before they attend the study or during the study.

....

Theme: Where Are You in the Movement?

....

Prayer: *Ever-present and attentive God, we know that you are with us as we aim to be your church. We pray for open hearts and minds as we learn and study about the ways you are working to make your church fresh for the next generation. Amen.*

....

Scripture Reading: 1 Corinthians 12:12-30
For just as the body is one and has many members, and all the members of the body, though many, are one body, so it is with Christ. For in the one Spirit we were all baptized into one body—Jews or Greeks, slaves or free—and we were all made to drink of one Spirit. Indeed, the body does not consist of one member but of many. If the foot would say, "Because I am not a hand, I do not belong to the body," that would not make it any less a part of the body. And if the ear would say, "Because I am not an eye, I do not belong to the body," that would not make it any less a part of the body. If the whole body were an eye, where would the hearing be? If the whole body were hearing, where would the sense of smell be? But as it is, God arranged the members in the body, each one of them, as he chose. If all were a single member, where would the body be? As it is, there are many members, yet one body. The eye cannot say to the hand, "I have no need of you," nor again the head to the feet, "I have no need of you." On the contrary, the members of the body that seem to be weaker are indispensable, and those members of the body that we think less honorable we clothe with greater honor, and our less respectable members are treated with greater respect; whereas our more respectable members do not need this. But God has so arranged the body, giving the greater honor to the inferior member, that there may be no dissension within the body, but the members

110

may have the same care for one another. If one member suffers, all suffer together with it; if one member is honored, all rejoice together with it.

Now you are the body of Christ and individually members of it. And God has appointed in the church first apostles, second prophets, third teachers; then deeds of power, then gifts of healing, forms of assistance, forms of leadership, various kinds of tongues. Are all apostles? Are all prophets? Are all teachers? Do all work miracles? Do all possess gifts of healing? Do all speak in tongues? Do all interpret? But strive for the greater gifts. And I will show you a still more excellent way.

Scripture Reflection

(Suggested answers are in *italics* after the question.)

1. What permission was Paul giving in this story? *(Paul was giving each the permission to participate, to claim their gifts and to use them toward the mission of God.)*

2. In Corinthians Paul reminds us that each of us have God-given gifts that help us participate in Christ's one body. What are some of the gifts you bring to the body of Christ?

3. While Paul was uplifting the various gifts that the people of God bring to make the body of Christ, he was also stressing that the gifts all work toward one mission. What is the mission of the church?

4. In this chapter we give examples of some of the players needed in forming a Fresh Expression. Where do you see yourself contributing to the mission of reaching new people, in new places and in new ways?

. . . .

Transition: *Paul knew he could not do everything himself, and he often encouraged all Christians to claim their spiritual gifts and use them toward the mission of God. Paul reminded his people that God needs all gifts and people and that we all need each other in this work of being the* *church. Fresh Expressions also aims at giving permission to new leaders and exploring the idea of the priesthood of all believers.*

....

Vocabulary: Each Bible study has a set of vocabulary terms to make sure everyone is speaking the same language and to give people language with which to speak about the church. Review the vocabulary terms with your small group at some point during your session.

- **Practitioner:** A person who leads a Fresh Expression. Someone who has the spiritual gifts of apostleship and compassion. Also known as a "pioneer" in Fresh Expressions UK.

- **Missional Mentor:** A person who will coach and encourage the practitioner.

- **Interpreter:** A person who is called to interpret the work of Fresh Expressions for a congregation or institutional body. This person may or may not participate in the Fresh Expression, but is able to help others understand the purpose and function of Fresh Expressions.

- **Steward:** A person who will seek and attend to the financial resources that sustain Fresh Expressions of church.

- **Permission-Giver:** A person of influence who is able to use their influence to give permission to a practitioner and/or a Fresh Expression.

- **Prayer Partner:** A person who prays for the Fresh Expression and all involved. This person may or may not be part of the Fresh Expression and may or may not be part of a local church.

- **Collaborator:** A person who is able to partner with the Fresh Expression through a variety of resources such as space, funds, or connecting points in the community.

Collaborators are found externally and internally in a local church and institution.

• **Person of Peace:** A person from the community who serves as a bridge between a Fresh Expression and the community.

....

Closing Thought: Where are you in Fresh Expressions? How might you let God use you to be part of the work of Fresh Expressions in your local community and/or church?

....

Closing Prayer: *God who is already at work through your Holy Spirit, empower each of us to use our gifts to be part of your work already happening in our communities and churches. May you guide each of us to understand what part you would have us play in the new thing you are doing. By your Holy Spirit, encourage us not only to listen or look but to follow you into our neighborhoods. Amen.*

6B. The Missionary Holy Spirit Goes Ahead of Us

Koinonia...is the fellowship of the Holy Spirit, across all barriers of race and class and sex and age. It was a new, emerging society out of a decaying society. This koinonia became the soul out of which the body the church, grew; it was the organism out of which the organization grew. Where you have the koinonia, you have the church; where you do not have the koinonia, you have an organization but not the church, except in name.

—E. Stanley Jones, *A Song of Ascents: A Spiritual Autobiography*

When Bishop Graham Cray, one of the pioneers of Fresh Expressions, described the existing church structures and cultural shifts in which present-day Christianity exists in England, the barriers seemed insurmountable. So many clergy and laity, many of them leaders, had settled into predictable rituals, and a growing sector beyond them seemed either bored with or cynical about the practice of faith. And then he paused and there was a twinkle in his eye: "But, you know, the missionary Holy Spirit is always going ahead of us!"

The simple call to "proclaim the gospel afresh" assumes that the Triune God indeed goes ahead of us. In the Wesleyan tradition, we describe this as "prevenient grace." Our missionary strategy doesn't presume to take God to people. We trust that God is already moving in the hearts of men and women, constantly engaging their minds with questions. At times the movement of the Holy Spirit is disruptive and public, like a Pentecostal storm; at other times there is a still, small voice—an awakening.

When the missionary Holy Spirit moves, we find ourselves caught up in something new; the Greek word is *koinonia*, often translated "fellowship" or "community." In his magisterial autobiography *A Song of Ascents*, E. Stanley Jones notes that Pentecost doesn't give birth to the church. The latter appears in Acts 8. Pentecost, he suggests, creates *koinonia*: "The believers devoted themselves to the apostles' teaching, to the community, to their shared meals and to their prayer" (Acts 2:42).

When the gospel is proclaimed afresh, we discover that walls crumble and relationships form. Fresh Expressions of church are one sign—and not the only sign—of the new creation. A part of the disillusionment of the "dones" and dechurched may be that many came searching for *koinonia* and couldn't find it.

The question at the heart of our reflection together is whether we can imagine a future that is both/and, a mixed ecology of vital traditional churches and life-giving gatherings of the nones and dones far outside the boundaries of Sunday morning at 11:00 a.m. Can clergy imagine serving traditional congregations while also developing new forms of community? Do judicatory leaders possess the courage to align resources with new constituencies who are not now in power? And, to push the question a bit further, can we imagine a Creator who loves diversity and desires that all come to the knowledge of the truth—in other words, a God who works through our churches but also at times beyond them?

In our roles as bishop and pastor, God has allowed us to see fresh expressions of church with our own eyes and to touch them with our own hands: in pubs, prisons, hotel dining rooms, dorm rooms, executive board rooms, and coffee shops; on street corners with day laborers; in a sex-offender village; beside a river on Sunday morning; and in a trailer park on Friday evening. We have witnessed Acts 2:42

in the persecution of Cuba, the secularism of urban England, the serenity of the Western North Carolina mountains, and the beautiful isolation of Florida's interior. Women and men have been bold enough to proclaim the gospel afresh, and *koinonia* happened.

In the lives of these leaders, laity, and clergy, we observed a holy risk and a profound trust. In each instance, they love the church. But they also know that God loves the world (John 3). In ministries that are both/and, in church parlors and third places, and among both members and disciples, cynics and seekers, these leaders are doing a new thing. The church, either through desperation or inspiration (or some holy combination of the two), comes to a place of blessing this movement; in the process she is herself transformed. This is the call to be a mission-shaped church.

We are grateful for conversations partners who have inspired us to think more deeply about a church shaped for mission. One of the most critical movements ahead of us will be a willingness to move beyond our cynicism about the church and our confusion about the culture. The invitation—the altar call, so to speak—is found in the preceding chapter, as you discern your own calling within the movement. This is a work in progress, but there is **a future with hope**. The One who began a good work in us will be faithful to complete it (Philippians 1:6).

So we ask you to join us in prayer:

May the Creating God baptize our imaginations to discover new forms of koinonia.

May the Saving Lord Jesus meet us wherever we break bread, and may our hearts once again burn within us.

May the Missionary Holy Spirit be poured out on all flesh, empowering us to proclaim the gospel afresh to next generations.

Amen!

Bible Study 12

Use this page as a template. Feel free to have participants read the chapter before they attend the study or during the study.

. . . .

Theme: The Missionary Holy Spirit Goes Ahead of Us

. . . .

Prayer: *Ever-present and attentive God, we know that you are with us as we aim to be your church. We pray for open hearts and minds as we learn and study about the ways you are working to make your church fresh for the next generation. Amen.*

. . . .

Scripture Reading: Acts 10
There was a man in Caesarea named Cornelius, a centurion in the Italian Company. He and his whole household were pious, Gentile God-worshippers. He gave generously to those in need among the Jewish people and prayed to God constantly. One day at nearly three o'clock in the afternoon, he clearly saw an angel from God in a vision. The angel came to him and said, "Cornelius!"

Startled, he stared at the angel and replied, "What is it, Lord?"

The angel said, "Your prayers and your compassionate acts are like a memorial offering to God. Send messengers to Joppa at once and summon a certain Simon, the one known as Peter. He is a guest of Simon the tanner, whose house is near the seacoast." When the angel who was speaking to him had gone, Cornelius summoned two of his household servants along with a pious soldier from his personal staff. He explained everything to them, then sent them to Joppa.

At noon on the following day, as their journey brought them close to the city, Peter went up on the roof to pray. He became hungry and wanted to eat. While others were preparing the meal, he had a visionary experience. He saw heaven opened up and something like a large linen sheet being lowered to the earth by its four corners. Inside the sheet were all kinds of four-legged animals, reptiles, and wild birds. A voice told him, "Get up, Peter! Kill and eat!"

Peter exclaimed, "Absolutely not, Lord! I have never eaten any-thing impure or unclean."

The voice spoke a second time, "Never consider unclean what God has made pure." This happened three times, then the object was suddenly pulled back into heaven.

Peter was bewildered about the meaning of the vision. Just then, the messengers sent by Cornelius discovered the whereabouts of Simon's house and arrived at the gate. Calling out, they inquired whether the Simon known as Peter was a guest there.

While Peter was brooding over the vision, the Spirit interrupted him, "Look! Three people are looking for you. Go downstairs. Don't ask questions; just go with them because I have sent them."

So Peter went downstairs and told them, "I'm the one you are looking for. Why have you come?"

They replied, "We've come on behalf of Cornelius, a centurion and righteous man, a God-worshipper who is well-respected by all Jewish people. A holy angel directed him to summon you to his house and to hear what you have to say." Peter invited them into the house as his guests.

The next day he got up and went with them, together with some of the believers from Joppa. They arrived in Caesarea the following day. Anticipating their arrival, Cornelius had gathered his relatives and close friends. As Peter entered the house, Cornelius met him and fell at his feet in order to honor him. But Peter lifted him up, saying, "Get up! Like you, I'm just a human." As they continued to talk, Peter went inside and found a large gathering of people. He said to them, "You all realize that it is forbidden for a Jew to associate or visit with outsiders. However, God has shown me that I should never call a person impure or unclean. For this reason, when you sent for me, I came without objection. I want to know, then, why you sent for me."

Cornelius answered, "Four days ago at this same time, three o'clock in the afternoon, I was praying at home. Suddenly a man in radiant clothing stood before me. He said, 'Cornelius, God has heard your prayers, and your compassionate acts are like a memorial offer-ing to him. Therefore, send someone to Joppa and summon Simon, who is known as Peter. He is a guest in the home of Simon the tan-ner, located near the seacoast.' I sent for you right away, and you were kind enough to come. Now, here we are, gathered in the presence of God to listen to everything the Lord has directed you to say."

Peter said, "I really am learning that God doesn't show partiality to one group of people over another. Rather, in every nation, whoever worships him and does what is right is acceptable to him. This is the message of peace he sent to the Israelites by proclaiming the good news through Jesus Christ: He is Lord of all! You know what happened throughout Judea, beginning in Galilee after the baptism John preached. You know about Jesus of Nazareth, whom God anointed with the Holy Spirit and endowed with power. Jesus traveled around doing good and healing everyone oppressed by the devil because God was with him. We are witnesses of everything he did, both in Judea and in Jerusalem. They killed him by hanging him on a tree, but God raised him up on the third day and allowed him to be seen, not by everyone but by us. We are witnesses whom God chose beforehand, who ate and drank with him after God raised him from the dead. He commanded us to preach to the people and to testify that he is the one whom God appointed as judge of the living and the dead. All the prophets testify about him that everyone who believes in him receives forgiveness of sins through his name."

While Peter was still speaking, the Holy Spirit fell on everyone who heard the word. The circumcised believers who had come with Peter were astonished that the gift of the Holy Spirit had been poured out even on the Gentiles. They heard them speaking in other languages and praising God. Peter asked, "These people have received the Holy Spirit just as we have. Surely no one can stop them from being baptized with water, can they?" He directed that they be baptized in the name of Jesus Christ. Then they invited Peter to stay for several days.

Scripture Reflection

(Suggested answers are in *italics* after the question.)

1. As a church we often identify who is in and who is out. Before Peter's transformation by the Holy Spirit, who did he believe was in God's saving grace and who was not? *(all people in)*

2. Whom do we identify as being in or out of God's saving grace? *(often the other, or persons outside our frames of experience)*

3. The Holy Spirit appeared to Peter in a vision. What was the vision? *(that all had been made clean)*

4. How did this vision play out in his interaction with Cornelius? *(He was accepted and baptized.)*

5. How did Peter's theology change after this vision?

6. Who was allowed in after this vision? *(all)*

. . . .

Transition: *The Holy Spirit used Peter to bring God's liberation and good news to all people. Fresh Expressions hopes to also provide an open door for any and all to enter in to God's story. In this chapter, we are challenged to explore the ways the church might have to change and clergy might have to change to make way for the work of the Spirit.*

. . . .

Book Reflection: Ask participants the following questions.

1. How has the church been negatively affected by our own actions and by outside critics?

2. How might the Holy Spirit be calling the church to a ministry of both/and?

3. How do you envision a church that both clings to tradition but opens its doors to innovation?

4. What hurdles do you anticipate in this work?

. . . .

Vocabulary: Each Bible study has a set of vocabulary terms to make sure everyone is speaking the same language and to give people language with which to speak about the church. Review the vocabulary terms with your small group at some point during your session.

- **Koinonia:** The Greek word often translated as fellowship and community.

. . . .

Closing Thought: This Bible study is not a task force or a committee but rather a group of people studying together Fresh Expressions and scripture. As you leave today, encourage your group NOT to go home and work on ways to fix the church. RATHER invite them to prayer and more study before you walk together toward solutions.

. . . .

Closing Prayer: *God who is always doing a new thing, help us to follow you with holy risk and profound trust so that more people can come into a trusting relationship with you. Amen.*

Citations and Further Reading

Ken Carter, "Rediscovering Ancient-Future Practices of Stewardship," *Faith and Leadership,* July 15, 2015.

Bob Hopkins and Freddy Hedley, *Coaching for Missional Leadership* (Sheffield, UK: ACPI, 2008).

Shannon Hopkins, "The Gamification of Innovation," *Faith and Leadership,* November 1, 2016.

Suzanne M. Johnson Vickberg and Kim Christfort, "Pioneers, Drivers, Integrators and Guardians," *Harvard Business Review,* March–April 2017: 50–56.

E. Stanley Jones, *A Song of Ascents: A Spiritual Autobiography* (Nashville: Abingdon, 1968).

Rowan Williams, "The 'Strength' of the Church Is Never Anything Other Than the Strength of the Risen Jesus," *Mixed Economy: The Journal of Fresh Expressions,* Autumn/Winter 2008–09: 13.

TO LEARN MORE ABOUT FRESH EXPRESSIONS

Recommended Online Resources

Fresh Expressions US
www.freshexpressionsus.org

Fresh Expressions UK
www. freshexpressions.org.uk

Florida Conference Fresh Expressions
www.flumc.org/freshexpressions

Ministry Incubators, Kenda Creasy Dean and Mark DeVries
www.ministryincubators.com

Path One of Discipleship Ministries of The United Methodist Church
www.umcdiscipleship.org

Recommended Books

Dietrich Bonhoeffer, *Life Together* (San Francisco: HarperOne, 2009).

Graham Cray, *Mission-Shaped Church: Church Planting and Fresh Expressions of Church in a Changing Context* (London: Church House Publishing, 2009).

Kenda Creasy Dean, *Almost Christian* (New York: Oxford, 2010).

Vincent J. Donovan, *Christianity Rediscovered* (Chicago: Orbis, 1978).

Elaine Heath and Scott Kisker, *Longing for Spring: A New Vision for Wesleyan Community,* New Monastic Library: Resources for Radical Discipleship (Eugene, OR: Wipf and Stock, 2010).

Lesslie Newbigin, *The Gospel in a Pluralistic Society* (Grand Rapids: Eerdmans, 1989).

CPSIA information can be obtained
at www.ICGtesting.com
Printed in the USA
LVHW080838210519
618286LV00002B/1/P